Study Guide

for

Kaplan's

A CHILD'S ODYSSEY
Child and Adolescent Development

Third Edition

Michael L. Jaffe
Kean University

Wadsworth
Thomson Learning™

Australia • Canada • Mexico • Singapore • Spain • United Kingdom • United States

ISBN 0-534-36934-0

For more information, contact
Wadsworth/Thomson Learning
10 Davis Drive
Belmont, CA 94002-3098
USA
http://www.wadsworth.com

International Headquarters
Thomson Learning
International Division
290 Harbor Drive, 2nd Floor
Stamford, CT 06902-7477
USA

UK/Europe/Middle East/South Africa
Thomson Learning
Berkshire House
168-173 High Holborn
London WC1V 7AA
United Kingdom

Asia
Thomson Learning
60 Albert Complex, #15-01
Singapore 189969

Canada
Nelson Thomson Learning
1120 Birchmount Road
Toronto, Ontario M1K 5G4
Canada

Study Guide

for

Kaplan's

A CHILD'S ODYSSEY
Child and Adolescent Development

Contents

READ ME FIRST

HOW TO STUDY YOUR TEXTBOOK

This study guide accompanies your textbook, <u>A Child's Odyssey</u> (3rd edition). This introduction presents you with helpful information about studying in general, and about studying <u>A Child's Odyssey</u> in particular. If you study this material carefully, you may be able to improve your study skills for all of your courses.

Every textbook presents a challenge: mastering new subject matter. Complex information cannot be digested without close examination and attention to detail. Careful reading alone may not be sufficient to accomplish this task. Many students report that, even after extended studying, they have difficulty retaining the massive amount of information presented in each textbook chapter.

This study guide contains study chapters that correspond to each chapter in the textbook. This guide can help you review and organize the material in the text so that you can learn and retain the information. Each study chapter contains chapter objectives, and a set of survey questions to guide your study of each chapter. There is blank space in the guide for you to answer each question. Important terms and concepts are presented, to be matched with their definitions. Self-tests with an answer key and challenge questions help you evaluate your study efforts. Chapter-related activities are also included, to be assigned by the instructor or to serve as ideas for term projects. Finally, there are activities based on the InfoTrac articles available to you through the InfoTrac website (http://www.infotrac-college.com/wadsworth).

Because this guide closely conforms to the material in <u>A Child's Odyssey</u>, it is recommended that you review a study chapter when the corresponding material is being covered in class. Preparing for class is an essential part of being a successful student and a successful test taker. Review recent lecture notes before class, and bring your text with you.

Participation in class discussions keeps your attention in the classroom and motivates you to understand the points being made by the teacher and other students. If you do not understand what is being said, ask questions. Try to relate what the instructor is saying to your own relevant experiences.

SUGGESTIONS ABOUT HOW TO STUDY

1. Class Preparation

Plan to spend between one and two hours of study time for each hour spent in class. It is recommended that you read the relevant material in a chapter before the topic is covered by the instructor.

Examine the survey questions in this guide briefly before class. They will provide additional perspective on what is being covered. After class, review your lecture notes, the relevant textbook chapter and **use this guide**.

2. Schedule

Study in relatively short sessions, each day. Don't cram. Short study sessions have been found to be more efficient than long, marathon sessions. Brief daily reviews of selected materials work wonders. The brevity (about 10 to 15 minutes) makes such reviews easier to initiate.

Pick a time of day when you are most alert (early morning for most of us), and if you are taking several courses, study the most difficult material first. Take a short break at least once an hour. Reward your efforts with a leisure activity that is pleasurable. Remember, it doesn't help to complain about your assignment. It is possible to make almost any material interesting, if you want to.

3. Setting

Find a place to study without distractions such as television, telephones, refrigerators and friends. The low noise level and the lighting found in libraries makes them an attractive place to study, and yet libraries are not so comfortable that you will become too relaxed or drowsy.

Whatever location you select, try to study in the same place each time. Familiarity of setting encourages learning. Posture is also important. Sit up in your chair. If you let yourself get bored, make your study experience more "physical" by standing or pacing as you study. Use mental imagery and your imagination to visualize the material-- this often improves retention.

4. SQ4R

There is an approach to studying known as the SQ4R method. Each letter stands for a particular step in studying that has been shown to be effective for most students. If you are not happy with your present study habits, or their results, experimenting with this technique will prove rewarding. Remember, the key to successful studying is **motivating** yourself to learn and retain the material.

S stands for survey -- briefly skim or survey the chapter and get a sense of what is being emphasized. What general topics are covered? The learning objectives stated at the beginning of each study guide chapter and the chapter summary found at the end of each textbook chapter should be read as part of the survey or introduction to the chapter.

Q stands for question -- survey the chapter again, this time asking yourself questions based on the headings or title of each section. (The survey questions found in this study guide and the true-false questions beginning each chapter in the textbook can also be used). This motivational device encourages you to read to answer your own questions rather than only those of the author. It helps you relate new concepts to ones that may already be familiar to you, a key step in learning.

R number 1 stands for read -- read the chapter using whatever study aids or techniques work for you. One way to make the material meaningful to you is to try to relate what you are learning in this course to what you already know about children.

R number 2 stands for "rite" -- some people find it useful to take notes as they read. Underlining is not as helpful as taking notes. When you take notes on a chapter, express the author's ideas in your own words.

R number 3 stands for recite -- as you read each section, or paragraph, restate the basic information in your **own** words without looking at the text. This key step transforms the author's behavior into your own behavior, an important aid to retention. Make a special attempt to recite and remember new concepts and unfamiliar vocabulary items.

R number 4 stands for review -- this step is used when studying for an exam. Rather than rereading the chapter, you now review the material you have previously learned using the preceding steps.

Parts of this guide that are particularly useful when studying for an examination include the important terms and concepts, to be matched with their definitions, and the challenge questions, which can help you organize and retain the main ideas of each chapter. Reviewing the material in study groups with other students and testing each other are also helpful ways of preparing for exams.

TAKING EXAMINATIONS

The purpose of a test is to demonstrate your mastery of the subject matter. Some tension before a test is normal, and desirable (it shows you care), but avoid placing yourself under intense pressure. Test anxiety usually reflects the expectation of danger- that something bad may happen to you, something you won't be able to handle. Self-induced test anxiety may impair your performance on the test. The better prepared you are, however, the less nervous you should feel.

Self-confidence, an important factor in successful test-taking, is promoted by sensible preparation and by rejecting self-defeating thoughts (e.g. "I'll never finish on time"; "What if I fail?"). Helpful self-statements include, "I am well-prepared," "I will do well if I concentrate," and "What do I have to do next?"

Don't exaggerate the importance of any particular exam. Tests are important, but they say nothing about your worthiness as a person! If test anxiety is a serious problem for you, consult your school's counseling center for help. Periodically taking deep breaths during exams helps you remain calm.

On testing day, arrive early to class. Use a pen because it writes more readably than a pencil. Pay attention to any spoken instructions, and read the written instructions carefully. First look over the entire exam and estimate the time priority for each question on the basis of its point value. Answer the easiest questions first, to build your confidence, and then answer the short answer questions.

Remember to write your answers to essay questions neatly, or your instructor may skip over some of your response. Answer the question that is asked, not the question you wanted asked. If you get stuck, think of something that is related; if you can't, move on to the next question. Resist the temptation to change answers unless you are confident of the change. Clearly indicate unanswered questions so you will find them easily when you want to return to them later.

The self-tests in the study guide provide you with a means of assessing your mastery of the subject matter after you study but before you are tested in class. Use any items you answer incorrectly to guide whatever additional studying might be necessary. Invent test questions of your own, putting them on flash cards with the answer on the back. Carry them with you and test yourself whenever you have spare time. If, after using this study guide, you still do poorly on tests, meet with your instructor to discuss this problem. Use the results of your exams to help you reevaluate your note taking strategy and your study strategy. If necessary, ask your instructor to help you find out what is working and what is not working for you.

I hope that this study guide will be used before, during, and after you study the textbook and class notes. Child development is an important and fascinating discipline. What you learn from this course should provide you with a valuable perspective for understanding and enjoying children.

The Study of Child and Adolescent Development

Chapter Objectives

After studying Chapter One of the text, you should be able to:

* define child development and describe the developmental perspective.

* distinguish between quantitative and qualitative change and give examples of each.

* give examples of how heredity and environment interact to produce developmental change.

* describe how the processes of maturation and learning lead to change.

* relate development to the cultural and subcultural contexts in which it occurs.

* describe how development reflects both economic and generational influences.

* evaluate how early and later life experiences might affect development.

* describe the stability of personality over the lifespan.

* analyze the reciprocal interactions between children and their caregivers.

* outline the relative advantages and disadvantages of different methods of research in developmental psychology, including naturalistic observation, the case study approach, and the survey approach.

* distinguish between correlations and causal relationships.

* discuss the pros and cons of cross-sectional and longitudinal research designs.

* describe the value of cross-cultural research and the difficulties involved in conducting cross-cultural research.

* discuss ethical considerations in experiments using human participants, including the use of deception.

* describe the potential benefits of studying developmental psychology.

Study Questions

Consider these questions <u>before</u> you read the chapter:

1. What is child psychology?

2. What is the difference between quantitative and qualitative change? Give one example of each.

3. The subject matter of developmental psychology is change. What role do each of the following play in producing developmental change?
   a. maturation
   b. the social environment
   c. learning

4. How do maturation and learning interact to produce change, using intelligence as an example?

5. For each of the following contexts, give one specific example of its potential influence on development:
   a. the family
   b. religious instruction
   c. school attendance
   d. neighborhood
   e. the media

6. What kinds of differences among subcultures could affect children's development?

7. How might racial or cultural stereotypes have a negative impact on minority children?

8. In what ways might individuals raised in the 1960s differ from those raised in the 1990s?

9. To what extent can later life experiences compensate for difficult early life experiences?

10. Are some personality traits more stable than others over the course of childhood?

11. In what sense do children "raise" their parents?

12. Do children develop in "leaps and bounds" or does change occur gradually (day by day)?

13. For each of the following research methods, describe the advantages and disadvantages:
    a. naturalistic observation
    b. case study
    c. survey
    d. experiment
    e. correlational approach

14. What is the difference between a cross-sectional and a longitudinal research design? Describe the advantages and disadvantages of each.

15. How do cross-cultural studies contribute to our understanding of development?

16. What types of ethical problems must researchers address when they work with children? What rights of children must always be respected?

Study Questions Review

After you have studied Chapter 1, fill in this section.

1. What is child psychology?

_____

_____

_____

_____

_____

2. What is the difference between quantitative and qualitative change? Give one example of each.

_____

_____

_____

_____

_____

3. The subject matter of developmental psychology is change. What role do each of the following play in producing developmental change?
   a. maturation
   b. the social environment
   c. learning

   _____
   _____
   _____
   _____
   _____
   _____
   _____
   _____
   _____

4. How do maturation and learning interact to produce change, using intelligence as an example?

   _____
   _____
   _____
   _____
   _____
   _____
   _____
   _____
   _____

5. For each of the following contexts, give one specific example of its potential influence on development:
   a. the family
   b. religious instruction
   c. school attendance
   d. neighborhood
   e. the media

   _____
   _____
   _____
   _____
   _____
   _____

6. What kinds of differences among subcultures could affect children's development?

_____

_____

_____

_____

7. How might racial or cultural stereotypes have a negative impact on minority children?

_____

_____

_____

_____

_____

_____

_____

_____

8. In what ways might individuals raised in the 1960s differ from those raised in the 1990s?

_____

_____

_____

_____

9. To what extent can later life experiences compensate for difficult early life experiences?

_____

_____

_____

_____

_____

_____

_____

10. Are some personality traits more stable than others over the course of childhood?

_____

_____

_____

_____

_____

11. In what sense do children "raise" their parents?

_____

_____

_____

_____

_____

_____

12. Do children develop in "leaps and bounds" or does change occur gradually (day by day)?

_____

_____

_____

_____

_____

13. For each of the following research methods, describe the advantages and disadvantages:
    a. naturalistic observation
    b. case study
    c. survey
    d. experiment
    e. correlational approach

_____

_____

_____

_____

_____

_____

_____

_____

_____

_____

_____

_____

_____

_____

_____

_____

14. What is the difference between a cross-sectional and a longitudinal research design? Describe the advantages and disadvantages of each.

_____

_____

_____

_____

_____

_____

_____

_____

15. How do cross-cultural studies contribute to our understanding of development?

_____

_____

_____

_____

_____

16. What types of ethical problems must researchers address when they work with children? What rights of children must always be respected?

_____

_____

_____

_____

_____

_____

_____

_____

Important Terms and Concepts

Match the term to its definition below

A. Experimental method_   R. Independent Variable _
B. Child development_   S. Reciprocal Interaction _
C. Replication _   T. Dependent Variable _
D. Sequential design_   U. Correlation _
E. Learning _
F. Dependent Variable _
G. Longitudinal Study _
H. Naturalistic Observation _
I. Qualitative Change _
J. Informed Consent _
K. Maturation _
L. Quantitative Change _
M. Survey Method _
N. Cohort Effect _
O. Time-lag study_
P. Cross-Sectional Design _
Q. Case Study _

Definitions

1. The scientific study of change throughout childhood

2. Changes that can be considered solely in terms of increases or decreases

3. Changes in function or process

4. Developmental changes that are due mainly to the unfolding of an individual's genetic plan

5. Relatively permanent changes in behavior due to interaction with the environment

6. The use of at least two cross-sections or two longitudinal analyses in the same study

7. A study that compares data presently gathered to data gathered at an earlier time, before the study was contemplated

8. Process by which an organism constantly affects and is affected by the environment

9. The repetition of a research study by other scientists

10. Observing people in their natural habitat

11. A research strategy using controls that allows the researcher to answer a particular question

12. Method of research in which a given person's behavior is studied over a long period of time

13. A method of research in which data are collected through written questionnaires or oral interviews

14. Controlled, systematic research that allows us to draw conclusions about cause and effect

15. The factor in a study which is manipulated by the researcher

16. The factor in a study which is measured by the experimenter, usually some measure of behavior

17. A measure of the degree to which two variables are related

18. A type of study in which groups of participants of different ages are compared

19. A type of study in which the same participants are observed or retested over a long period of time

20. The effect of belonging to a particular generation or period of history

21. Telling participants everything about a study they would need to know in order to decide whether to participate

Answers

A. 11	B. 1	C. 9
D. 6	E. 5	F. 16
G. 19	H. 10	I. 3
J. 21	K. 4	L. 2
M. 13	N. 20	O. 7
P. 18	Q. 12	R. 15
S. 8	T. 16	U. 17

Self-test: Multiple Choice

1. In a ----- study, researchers compare children of different ages.
a. case
b. cross-sectional
c. longitudinal
d. correlational

2. Child development is the study of
a. growth.
b. maturation.
c. children.
d. change.

3. Relatively permanent changes in behavior that result from interacting with the environment are called
a. learning.
b. development.
c. growth.
d. puberty.

4. Which research method studies a particular person over an extended period?
a. naturalistic observation
b. experiment
c. case study
d. survey method

5. The most powerful research method, in terms of explaining behavior, is the
a. field study.
b. case study.
c. survey.
d. experiment.

6. Which one of the following is an independent variable?
a. amount eaten
b. type of food offered
c. rate of eating
d. number of eyeblinks

7. A cohort effect reflects the effect of
a. generational similarities.
b. age differences.
c. malnutrition.
d. cultural differences.

8. A qualitative change is illustrated by
a. physical growth.
b. the onset of menstruation.
c. an increase in vocabulary.
d. a decrease in bedwetting.

9. Which one of the following is most dependent on environmental influence?
a. maturation
b. growth
c. puberty
d. learning

10. If a researcher accurately describes exactly what he or she did in conducting a given study, other researchers can then --- the study.
a. criticize
b. expand
c. replicate
d. all of the above

Self-test: True-False

__ 1. If 12-year-olds in one school system are surveyed about their views about premarital sex, the results of the survey cannot be generalized to 12-year-olds in a different school system.

__ 2. Laboratory research is usually performed under realistic circumstances.

__ 3. Longitudinal studies are more time-consuming than are cross-sectional studies.

__ 4. Research with children requires fewer ethical considerations than research with adults.

__ 5. Deception in research can never be justified.

__ 6. The manipulation of an independent variable is a critical part of a survey.

__ 7. Child development is the scientific study of maturation.

__ 8. Later experiences can at least partially compensate for poor early experiences.

__ 9. Maturational changes are relatively independent of environmental influences.

__ 10. Intelligence reflects both learning and biology.

__ 11. Children influence their parents as much as their parents influence them.

__ 12. Correlations can only be positive.

Answers

Multiple Choice

1. B	6. B
2. D	7. A
3. A	8. B
4. C	9. D
5. D	10. D

True False

1. T	7. F
2. F	8. T
3. T	9. T
4. F	10. T
5. F	11. T
6. F	12. F

Challenge Questions

1. Select three behavioral changes that you might observe in a preschool child (such as feeding herself) and speculate about the relative roles played by maturation and learning in their development.

_____

_____

_____

_____

_____

_____

_____

_____

_____

_____

2. Distinguish between qualitative and quantitative changes in development, using the following changes as examples:

a. learning to walk

_____

_____

b. acquiring language

_____
_____
_____
_____

c. getting good grades in elementary school

_____
_____
_____
_____
_____
_____
_____
_____

3. How might extreme environmental factors such as poverty, malnutrition, and child abuse affect maturational development?

_____
_____
_____
_____
_____
_____
_____

4. Outline the steps of a research study that would test whether bottle feeding or breast feeding an infant leads to faster weight gain. What type of study would you choose? What variables would you study? Who would your participants be? What ethical considerations would have to be addressed?

_____
_____
_____
_____

_____
_____
_____
_____
_____
_____

Chapter Activities

1. Design and conduct a simple naturalistic observation study. Think of a question about child development you would like to answer, such as "Do fathers play differently with their young children than mothers do?" Then visit a local park or playground and unobtrusively observe fathers and mothers interacting with their children.

Record data about specific observations (e.g. Do fathers push their children higher on the swings? Do mothers stay closer to their children?). If possible, work in pairs; you and a classmate can record your observations independently, and then compare notes. What problems do you find with this method of observation? Report your findings.

2. Do parents in different subcultures parent differently? Construct a questionnaire tapping the beliefs, values, and behaviors of parents. For example, inquire about how they handle discipline encounters, set limits on television watching, and their opinions about school, homework, and achievement. After having your instructor approve the questions, administer the questionnaire to parents in different subcultures, such as African American, Latino, and Asian. Analyze your findings and report on similarities and differences among the various subcultural groups.

3. Compare the following two research articles from **InfoTrac** regarding: the type of research design; use of cross sectional or longitudinal design; research participants; the research hypothesis; ethical considerations; measuring instruments used; the main findings; strengths and weaknesses of each study; and the investigators' interpretations of the significance of their findings
  1. Huba, M.E., Ramisetty-Mikler, S. (1995). The language skills and concepts of early and nonearly readers. *Journal of Genetic Psychology, 156*, p. 313 (19).
  2. Olson, H.C., Streissguth, A.P., Sampson, P.D., Barr, H.M., Bookstein, F.L. & Thiede, K. (1997). Association of prenatal alcohol exposure with behavioral and learning problems in early adolescence. *Journal of the American Academy of Child and Adolescent Psychiatry, 36,* p. 1187 (8).

Perspectives *on* Child Development

Chapter Objectives

After studying Chapter Two, you should be able to:

* describe why theory is important in developmental psychology.

* distinguish between a good theory and a bad theory.

* distinguish between stage and non-stage theories.

* describe the major concepts of Piaget's theory including the four stages of cognitive development.

* outline Freud's psychoanalytic theory and describe the five psychosexual stages.

* compare Erikson's psychosocial theory to Freud's psychosexual theory and describe Erikson's eight stages of development.

* describe the basic concepts and principles of the behavioral approach, including classical and operant conditioning.

* give examples of classical and operant conditioning.

* discuss social-learning theory and the process by which people learn through observation.

* describe the basic assumptions and principles of the information processing model of cognitive development.

* analyze the role that social interactions play in children's development, according to Vygotsky.

* describe the many types of environments that children inhabit, as described by ecological theory.

* summarize the strengths and weaknesses of the major theories presented in this chapter.

Study Questions

Consider these questions **before** you read the chapter:

1. What is it about developmental theories that can help us understand why children turn out the way that they do?

2. How can we tell a good (useful) theory from a bad one? List four criteria of a useful theory.

3. For each of the following theorists or theories of development, cite one major concept used to understand development, and one criticism of the concept:

   a. Piaget
   b. Freud
   c. Erikson
   d. Behavioral (conditioning) approaches
   e. Social learning theory
   f. Information processing approach
   g. Bronfenbrenner's ecological theory
   h. Vygotsky's sociocultural theory
   I. Chaos theory

4. According to Piaget, how do children resolve discrepancies between what they know and what they are experiencing?

5. In everyday language, what aspects of human personality was Freud describing as the id, the ego, and the superego? According to Freud, what role does pleasure play in the development of personality?

6. What did Erikson mean by a life crisis?

7. Describe the similarities and differences between Freud's and Erikson's theories of development.

8. How is the information processing view of cognitive development related to our understanding of how computers work?

9. Regarding conditioning models of development,
   a. How does classical conditioning help us understand the emotional life of children?
   b. How might a parent unintentionally encourage defiant behavior?
   c. How can parents use extinction to discourage antisocial behavior?

10. How does the parental retort, "Do as I say, not as I do" relate to the Social Learning approach to development?

11. According to Vygotsky, how do cultures transmit behaviors and values from one generation to the next?

12. To what extent does ecological theory incorporate the other models of development described in this chapter?

13. Which one of the models described in this chapter makes the most sense to you? Defend your answer.

Study Questions Review

After you have studied Chapter Two, fill in this section.

1. What is it about developmental theories that can help us understand why children turn out the way that they do?

_____

_____

_____

_____

_____

_____

_____

_____

_____

_____

2. How can we tell a good (useful) theory from a bad one? List four criteria of a useful theory.

_____

_____

_____

_____

_____

3. For each of the following theorists or theories of development, cite one major concept used to understand development, and one criticism of the concept:

    a. Piaget
    b. Freud
    c. Erikson
    d. Behavioral (conditioning) approaches
    e. Social learning theory
    f. Information processing approach
    g. Bronfenbrenner's ecological theory
    h. Vygotsky's sociocultural theory
    i. Chaos theory

_____
_____
_____
_____
_____
_____
_____
_____
_____
_____
_____
_____
_____
_____
_____

4. According to Piaget, how do children resolve discrepancies between what they know and what they are experiencing?

_____
_____
_____
_____
_____

5. In everyday language, what aspects of human personality was Freud describing as the id, the ego, and the superego? What role does pleasure play in the development of personality?

_____

_____

_____

_____

_____

_____

_____

_____

6. What did Erikson mean by a life crisis?

_____

_____

_____

_____

_____

7. Describe the similarities and differences between Freud's and Erikson's theories of development.

_____

_____

_____

_____

_____

_____

_____

_____

_____

_____

8. How is the information processing view of cognitive development related to our understanding of how computers work?

_____

_____

_____

_____

_____

9. Regarding conditioning models of development,
    a. How does classical conditioning help us understand the emotional life of children?
    b. How might a parent unintentionally encourage defiant behavior?
    c. How can parents use extinction to discourage antisocial behavior?

_____

_____

_____

_____

_____

_____

_____

_____

_____

10. How does the parental retort, "Do as I say, not as I do" relate to the Social Learning approach to development?

_____

_____

_____

_____

_____

11. According to Vygotsky, how do cultures transmit behaviors and values from one generation to the next?

_____

_____

_____

_____

_____

12. To what extent does ecological theory incorporate the other models of development described in this chapter?

_____

_____

_____

_____

_____

_____

_____

_____
_____
_____

13. Which one of the models described in this chapter makes the most sense to you? Defend your answer.

_____
_____
_____
_____
_____
_____
_____
_____
_____
_____

Important Terms and Concepts

Match the term to its definition below

A. Preoperational __
B. Displacement __
C. Ego __
D. Stimulus generalization __
E. Phallic stage __
F. Id __
G. Assimilation __
H. Discrimination __
I. Electra complex __
J. Superego __
K. Schema __
L. Extinction __
M. Epigenetic principle __
N. Libido __
O. Anal stage __
P. Conscious mind __
Q. Classical conditioning __
R. Operation __
S. Genital stage __
T. Sensorimotor stage __
U. Repression __
V. Accommodation __
W. Oral stage __
X. Preconscious __
Y. Defense mechanism __
Z. Equilibration __

AA. Concrete operations __
BB. Oedipal complex __
CC. Unconscious __
DD. Psychosexual stage __
EE. Formal operations __
FF. Ego ideal __
GG. Object permanence __
HH. Latency phase __
II. Reality principle __
JJ. Eros __
KK. Pleasure principle __
LL. Behaviorist __
MM. Reinforcer __
NN. Information processing theory __
OO. Social learning theory __

Definitions

1. A method of dealing with the environment that can be generalized to many situations

2. An internalized action that is part of the child's cognitive structure

3. The process by which information is altered to fit into one's already existing cognitive structures

4. The process by which one's existing cognitive structures are altered to fit new information

5. The first stage in Piaget's theory, in which a child discovers the world using the senses and motor activity

6. The second stage in Piaget's theory, during which children cannot understand logical concepts such as conservation

7. The third stage in Piaget's theory, in which the child develops the ability to conserve and becomes less egocentric

8. The final stage in Piaget's theory, in which the adolescent develops the ability to deal with abstractions and engage in scientific logical thought

9. Freudian term for thoughts and memories of which a person is aware

10. Freudian terms for thoughts and memories that, although not in awareness, can easily become conscious

11. Freudian term for memories that lie beyond normal awareness

12. The process by which an emotion is transferred from one object or person to another, more acceptable, substitute

13. The portion of the mind in Freudian theory which serves as the depository for wishes and desires

14. In Piagetian theory, the process by which children seek a balance between what they know and what they are experiencing

15. The part of the mind in Freudian theory which mediates between the real world and the desires of the id

16. The knowledge that objects exist even if they are outside one's field of vision

17. The part of the mind in Freudian theory which includes a set of principles, violation of which leads to feelings of guilt

18. The individual's positive and desirable standards of conduct, according to Freudian theory

19. An automatic and unconscious process that reduces or eliminates feelings of anxiety or emotional conflict

20. A defense mechanism in which memories are barred from consciousness

21. In Freudian theory, the energy emanating from the sex instinct

22. Stages in Freud's developmental theory

23. Freud's first psychosexual stage, in which pleasure is centered on the oral cavity (the mouth)

24. Freud's second psychosexual stage, in which pleasure is centered on the anal cavity

25. The third psychosexual stage, according to Freud, in which pleasure is centered on the genital areas

26. The conflict during the phallic stage in which a boy experiences romantic feelings toward his mother

27. The female equivalent of the Oedipal complex, in which a girl experiences romantic feelings toward her father

28. Freud's fourth psychosexual stage, in which pleasure is not centered on any particular part of the body

29. Freud's final psychosexual stage, during which heterosexual behavior develops

30. The preset developmental principle in Erikson's theory emphasizing the role of maturation and environmental challenges

31. A learning process in which a neutral stimulus comes to elicit a response already elicited by another stimulus

32. The tendency of an organism that has learned to associate a certain behavior with a particular stimulus to show this behavior in the presence of other similar stimuli

33. The process by which a person learns to differentiate among stimuli

34. The weakening and disappearance of a learned response

35. In Freudian theory, the positive, constructive sex instinct

36. According to Freud, the process by which the ego satisfies the organism's needs in a socially appropriate manner

37. The principle governing the id, which involves achieving satisfaction as quickly as possible

38. A psychologist who explains behavior in terms of the processes of learning and other environmental factors

39. An approach to understanding cognition based on the input, processing, output computer model

40. The theoretical view that people learn by observing and imitating other people's behaviors

41. A stimulus that increases the probability of the response it follows

Answers

A. 6	B. 12	C. 15
D. 32	E. 25	F. 13
G. 3	H. 33	I. 27
J. 17	K. 1	L. 34
M. 30	N. 21	O. 24
P. 9	Q. 31	R. 2
S. 29	T. 5	U. 20
V. 4	W. 23	X. 10
Y. 19	Z. 14	AA. 7
BB.26	CC.11	DD. 22
EE. 8	FF. 18	GG. 16
HH. 28	II. 36	JJ. 35
KK. 37	LL. 38	MM.41
NN. 39	OO.40	

Self-test: Multiple Choice

1. Which one of the following was not cited as a criterion for assessing theories?
a. testability
b. predictability
c. conventionality
d. inclusiveness

2. Non-stage theorists
a. view development in terms of age-related periods.
b. view development as a step-like progression.
c. view development as a continuous process.
d. see children's development occurring in "leaps and bounds."

3. According to Freud, feelings of guilt are the product of the
a. id.
b. superego.
c. ego.
d. environment.

4. Defense mechanisms protect us from
a. criticism.
b. infections.
c. anxiety.
d. depression.

5. According to Freud, fixation at the oral stage of development may lead to
a. impotence.
b. dependency.
c. confusion.
d. stuttering.

6. A boy's longing for his mother suggests Freud's concept of
a. the Electra complex.
b. the Oedipal complex.
c. the ego ideal.
d. repression.

7. Piaget had children fill glasses of water
a. because he was thirsty.
b. to assess their muscle coordination.
c. to test their understanding of conservation.
d. to evaluate their willingness to cooperate.

8. According to Erikson, the developmental challenge associated with adolescence is
a. trust vs. mistrust.
b. autonomy vs. shame and doubt.
c. identity vs. role confusion.
d. integrity vs. despair.

9. According to Piaget, what children know about the world is organized as
a. schemata.
b. images.
c. operations.
d. reflexes.

10. Which one of the following theorists does not advocate a stage theory of development?
a. Bandura
b. Piaget
c. Freud
d. Erikson

11. Learning through observation is emphasized by
a. Behavioral approaches.
b. Social learning approaches.
c. Piaget.
d. Information processing approaches.

12. The concept of limited capacity is associated with
a. Piaget.
b. Skinner.
c. Erikson.
d. the information processing view of development.

13. Pairing a neutral stimulus with a stimulus that already elicits a particular response is called
a. classical conditioning.
b. operant conditioning.
c. assimilation.
d. generalization.

14. The use of rewards to encourage desirable behavior in children was advocated mainly by
a. Piaget.
b. Erikson.
c. Freud.
d. the behaviorists.

15. The first step in the process of imitation is
a. retention in memory.
b. paying attention.
c. using stored information.
d. reinforcement.

16. The concept of self-efficacy resembles that of
a. equilibration.
b. acculturation.
c. self-confidence.
d. microsystem.

17. The importance of social context in learning was most emphasized by
a. Vygotsky.
b. Piaget.
c. Bronfenbrenner.
d. Darwin.

Self-test: True-False Questions

_1. Scientists create theories because theories are useful.

_2. A theory can never be proven to be true.

_3. Freud claimed the id develops by the end of the first year.

_4. The validity of Freud's basic concepts is still being debated by psychologists.

_5. The superego is analogous to one's conscience.

_6. Erikson described ten stages of psychosocial development.

_7. Operant conditioning involves the pairing of a neutral stimulus with an eliciting stimulus.

_8. A toddler calling a strange man "daddy" exemplifies generalization.

_9. Much of what children learn from their caregivers is based on observational learning.

_10. Information-processing theory focuses on observable behavior.

_11. A reinforcer increases the likelihood of the response it follows.

_12. The first step in imitation is paying attention to the model.

_13. Vygotsky maintained that culture is transmitted from one generation to the next through operant conditioning.

_14. According to Bronfenbrenner, many different environments influence a child simultaneously.

Answers

Multiple Choice

1. C	7. C	13. A
2. C	8. C	14. D
3. B	9. A	15. B
4. C	10. A	16. C
5. D	11. B	17. A
6. B	12. D	

True-False

1. T	8. T
2. T	9. T
3. F	10. F
4. T	11. T
5. T	12. T
6. F	13. F
7. F	14. T

Challenge Questions

1. According to Freud's theory, many of our actions are governed by unconscious motives, such as selfish, sexual, and aggressive impulses and desires. If you were aware of these impulses, according to Freud, you would presumably find them unacceptable and even threatening. Does this make it difficult to accept Freud's proposition? Is it easier to accept if you apply it to someone else's behavior? Is it easier to deny than admit that you are very angry at someone you care for?

_____
_____
_____
_____
_____
_____
_____
_____
_____
_____
_____
_____

2. Children often say and do things that adults consider "cute." According to Piaget's point of view, are children simply less informed about our world, or are there fundamental differences between how children and adults make sense of their experiences?

_____
_____
_____
_____
_____
_____
_____
_____
_____
_____

3. Behavioral approaches to development emphasize the role that reward and punishment play in shaping behavior and personality. How modifiable are children by environmental influences (e.g., family, education), compared to innate or biological determinants of personality?

_____
_____

_____
_____
_____
_____
_____
_____
_____

4. In teaching a five-year-old to ride a two-wheel bicycle, how much would you depend on
   a. rewards
   b. imitation
   c. instruction
   d. punishment or disapproval

_____
_____
_____
_____
_____
_____
_____
_____
_____
_____

Chapter Activities

1. Select a child you know well, and examine and interpret aspects of that child's personality using any three of the theories described in this chapter. What types of questions and observations are suggested by each theory? Which theories are more useful in understanding your observations of this particular child? Report your findings.

2. The **InfoTrac** reading by Geisert and Futrell (1996), Free will: A human, fuzzy, chaotic process (In *The Humanist, 56,* p. 26 (4)) argues that humans have free will insofar as we have the ability to process the dozens of factors that typically influence our decisions and we usually arrive at a reasonable choice. Based on your reading of this article, contrast the deterministic and free will models of human behavior and state your opinion about which makes more sense to you. Describe how an important decision that you recently made was either determined or free of obvious influence.

3. Based on Grossman and Till's (1998) **InfoTrac** article, The persistence of classically conditioned brand attitudes (*Journal of Advertising, 27,* p. 23 (9)), select five ads from TV or magazines and describe their use of classical conditioning principles to sell a product.

Mechanisms *of* Change: Genetic *and* Environmental Interaction

Chapter Objectives

After studying Chapter Three of the text, you should be able to:

* convey the basics of genetic transmission (heredity) applying key terms, including chromosome, dominant and recessive traits, phenotype, genotype, and polygenic inheritance.

* describe why males are more susceptible than females to sex-linked disorders.

* define heritability and interpret heritability figures.

* describe the heritability of physical characteristics, including the rate of development.

* describe how twin and adoption studies can clarify the relative influence on development of heredity and environment.

* analyze the relationship between heredity, temperament, child rearing, and child personality.

* discuss why children in the same family usually have such different personalities.

* analyze the relationship between heredity, culture, and intelligence.

* describe the heritability of genetic disorders such as cystic fibrosis, Tay-Sachs disease, and PKU.

*discuss the role of chromosomal abnormalities in Down syndrome, Turner's syndrome, and Klinefelter's syndrome.

* discuss the possible role of heredity in alcoholism and in severe mental disorders such as schizophrenia.

* describe the role the genetic counselor can play in helping prospective parents make good decisions about reproduction.

* describe how environmental factors mediate the way genes express themselves.

Study Questions

Consider these questions **before** you read the chapter:

1. Why do psychologists study both biological and environmental influences on development?

2. How much of "human nature" is inherited? How much reflects socialization and education?

3. Can inherited traits be modified?

4. Should parents have the right to decide the gender of their child?

5. How is the sex of a child determined genetically?

6. Distinguish between
   a. dominant and recessive traits.
   b. genotype and phenotype.
   c. polygenic and multifactorial traits.

7. How might a woman who does not suffer from color blindness pass this disorder on to her son?

8. Why do children with the same biological parents often have little or no physical resemblance to each other? Why are siblings usually so different in personality?

9. How are identical twins different from fraternal twins genetically and physically?

10. Are adopted children more similar in personality to their biological parents or adoptive parents?

11. How might a child's temperament affect the parent-child relationship?

12. What role does heredity play in the development of each of the following?
    a. agression
    b. personality
    c. intelligence

13. How might genetic information be misused?

14. What are the genetic bases and major features of
   a. Tay-Sachs disease?
   b. phenylketonuria (PKU)?
   c. sickle cell anemia?
   d. Down Syndrome?
   e. schizophrenia
   f. alcoholism

15. How might a child's genes contribute to the type of family environment she experiences?

Study Questions Review

   After you have studied Chapter Three, fill in this section.

1. Why do psychologists study both biological and environmental influences on development?

_____

_____

_____

_____

_____

_____

_____

2. How much of "human nature" is inherited? How much reflects socialization and education?

_____

_____

_____

_____

_____

_____

_____

_____

_____

_____

_____

_____

3. Can inherited traits be modified? Explain.

_____
_____
_____
_____
_____

4. Should parents have the right to decide the gender of their child? Defend your answer.

_____
_____
_____
_____
_____
_____
_____
_____
_____
_____

5. How is the sex of a child determined genetically?

_____
_____
_____
_____

6. Distinguish between
    a. dominant and recessive traits.
    b. genotype and phenotype.
    c. polygenic and multifactorial traits.

_____
_____
_____
_____
_____
_____
_____
_____
_____
_____

_____
_____
_____
_____

7. How might a woman who does not suffer from color blindness pass this disorder on to her son?

_____
_____
_____
_____
_____

8. Why do children with the same biological parents often have little or no physical resemblance to each other? Why are siblings usually so different in personality?

_____
_____
_____
_____
_____
_____
_____
_____
_____
_____

9. How are identical twins different from fraternal twins genetically and physically?

_____
_____
_____
_____
_____
_____
_____
_____
_____
_____

10. Are adopted children more similar in personality to their biological parents or adoptive parents?

_____
_____

_____
_____
_____

11. How might a child's temperament affect the parent-child relationship?

_____
_____
_____
_____
_____

12. What role does heredity play in the development of each of the following?
    a. agression
    b. personality
    c. intelligence

_____
_____
_____
_____
_____
_____
_____
_____
_____
_____
_____
_____
_____

13. How might genetic information be misused?

_____
_____
_____
_____

14. What are the genetic bases and major features of
    a. Tay-Sachs disease?
    b. phenylketonuria (PKU)?
    c. sickle cell anemia?
    d. Down Syndrome?

e. schizophrenia
f. alcoholism

_____
_____
_____
_____
_____
_____
_____
_____
_____
_____
_____
_____

15. How might a child's genes contribute to the type of family environment she experiences?

_____
_____
_____
_____
_____
_____
_____
_____
_____
_____
_____

Important Terms and Concepts

Match the term to its definition below

A. Readiness__
B. Concordance rate __
C. Meiosis __
D. Carrier __
E. Phenotype __
F. Heritability __
G. Gametes __
H. Sex chromosome __
I. Schizophrenia __
J. Gene __
K. Monozygotic (identical) twins __
L. Sex linked traits __
M. Dominant traits __

N. Cystic fibrosis __
O. Tay Sachs disease __
P. Behavior genetics __
Q. Chromosomes __
R. Phenylketonuria (PKU) __
S. Recessive traits __
T. Sex selection __
U. Genotype __
V. Multifactorial traits __
W. Dizygotic (fraternal) twins __

Definitions

1. A term used to describe how much of the variation seen in any particular trait is due to heredity

2. The study of how genetic endowment influences behavior

3. The basic unit of heredity

4. Rod-shaped structures that carry the genes

5. The scientific term for the sex cells

6. The process by which sex cells divide to form two cells, each containing 23 chromosomes

7. Techniques that allow couples to choose the sex of their child

8. Twins that develop from one fertilized egg and have an identical genetic structure

9. Twins resulting from fertilization of two eggs by two different sperm and whose genes are no more similar than any other pair of siblings

10. The twenty-third pair of chromosomes, which determines the sex of the organism

11. Traits that require the presence of only one gene

12. Traits that require the presence of two genes

13. A severe genetic disease marked by digestive and respiratory problems

14. A person who possesses a particular gene or group of genes for a trait, who does not show the trait but who can pass it on to his or her children

15. The genetic configuration of the individual

16. The observable characteristics of the organism

17. Traits that are influenced both by genes and the environment

18. Traits that are inherited through genes found on the sex chromosomes

19. The point in development at which a child has the necessary skills to master a new challenge

20. A fatal genetic disease most commonly found in Jews who can trace their lineage to Eastern Europe

21. A recessive genetic disorder marked by the inability to digest a particular protein and possibly leading to mental retardation

22. A severe mental disorder marked by hallucinations, delusions, and emotional disturbances

23. The degree of similarity between twins on any particular trait

Answers

A. 19	B. 23	C. 6
D. 14	E. 16	F. 1
G. 5	H. 10	I. 22
J. 3	K. 8	L. 18
M. 11	N. 13	O. 20
P. 2	Q. 4	R. 21
S. 12	T. 7	U. 15
V. 17	W. 9	

Self-test: Multiple Choice

1. A trait with very low, if any, heritability is
a. intelligence.
b. computer literacy.
c. eye color.
d. handedness.

2. The normal human cell contains how many chromosomes?
a. 23
b. 46
c. 92
d. 50,000

3. The specific composition of a person's genes is referred to as his or her
a. genotype.
b. concordance rate.
c. phenotype.
d. gametes.

4. Which one of the following traits is sex-linked?
a. hemophilia
b. eye color
c. skin color
d. freckles

5. A treatable inherited disorder involving the ability to digest a protein is called
a. Huntington's Chorea.
b. Tay-Sachs disease.
c. Phenylketonuria (PKU).
d. Turner's syndrome.

6. Children with Down Syndrome usually have
a. an unusual appearance.
b. one extra chromosome.
c. an intellectual impairment.
d. all of the above.

7. "Slow to warm up" children
a. do not respond well to changes in their environment.
b. are generally happy, flexible, and regular.
c. are intense, demanding, and inflexible.
d. adjust best to strict parenting.

8. Genetic counselors help people by
a. diagnosing and describing particular disorders.
b. calculating the probabilities that a disorder will be transmitted to offspring.
c. helping prospective parents reach a decision about continuing a pregnancy.
d. all of the above.

9. The basic units of heredity are the
a. chromosomes.
b. gametes.
c. sperm and egg.
d. genes.

10. For each of the following traits, indicate whether the major contributor to the trait is heredity (H), environment (E) or whether both (B) have a significant influence.

a. Temperament __
b. Intelligence __
c. Facial appearance __
d. Political opinions __
e. Language acquisition __
f. Schizophrenia __
g. Alcoholism __

Self-test: True-False Questions

__ 1. Heritability is a measure of the variation of a trait due to heredity.

__2. The basic unit of heredity is DNA.

__3. Dominant traits will be expressed even if one member of the gene pair is recessive.

__4. Young children's temperaments have little genetic input.

__5. Fraternal twins can be of the opposite sex.

__6. An inherited defect in the structure of red blood cells is called Tay Sachs disease.

__7. Females are born with all of the eggs they will ever have.

__8. Parents can modify certain infant behaviors by changing their parenting styles.

__9. If both parents are right-handed, it is impossible for their children to be left-handed.

__10. Genetic counselors will insist that a couple terminate their pregnancy if the fetus has been shown to have chromosomal abnormalities.

Answers

Multiple Choice

1. B	9. D
2. B	10. a. H
3. A	b. B
4. A	c. H
5. C	d. E
6. D	e. B
7. A	f. B
8. D	g. B

True-False

1. T
2. F
3. T
4. F
5. T
6. F
7. T
8. T
9. F
10. F

Challenge Questions

1. Abortion remains a controversial issue in our society. Some people maintain that a fetus is part of its mother's body, so she has the right to decide its fate. Others believe that the fetus has rights of its own, independent of its mother. What do you think, and why?

_____
_____
_____
_____
_____
_____
_____
_____

2. If you possessed a gene for a harmful trait like hemophilia, would it affect your decision to have a child? What steps would you take to make a more informed decision?

_____
_____
_____
_____
_____
_____
_____

3. The more we learn about genes, the closer we come to controlling the genetic process. Do you think parents should be able to select certain characteristics, such as their child's sex, size, eye color or temperament? How might such selections change our society?

_____
_____
_____
_____
_____
_____
_____
_____
_____

4. Brown eyes are dominant over blue. Can two brown-eyed parents bear a blue-eyed child? Explain. Can two blue-eyed parents bear a brown-eyed child? What might be the implications of the latter occurrence?

Chapter Activities

1. Interview parents regarding their perceptions of how their children resemble or do not resemble them. Determine whether parents perceive physical (e.g., size, facial appearance) and psychological (e.g., opinions, mannerisms, abilities) similarities between themselves and their children.
You may want to compose a checklist of possible traits. See whether mothers and fathers agree with each other's perceptions of their children. Ask the parents to discuss the source of the resemblances-- do they understand what is heritable and what is not? Report your findings.

2. Eberstadt's (1998) **InfoTrac** article, What are parents for? (*Commentary, 106,* p. 17), responds to Judith Harris's premise that peers exert more influence on children's development than parents do. Describe your response to this controversial issue. Should parents be held responsible for how their children "turn out"? (Keep in mind that parents are legally responsible for their children's behavior until a child is 18 years old). How might the age of a child or adolescent moderate parental influence? Do we know why children turn out as they do? What is Eberstadt's position?

3. Regarding Pike and Plomin's **InfoTrac** article, Importance of nonshared environmental factors for childhood and adolescent psychopathology (In the *Journal of the American Academy of Child and Adolescent Psychiatry, 35,* p. 560), what do the authors mean by nonshared environment? To what extent do siblings share the same family environment? To what extent are they being raised by "different parents"? How do the authors use the concepts of shared and nonshared environments to account for differences in how siblings adjust?

Prenatal Development *and* Birth

Chapter Objectives

After studying Chapter Four of the text, you should be able to:

* describe prenatal development from the germinal through the embryonic and fetal stages.

* discuss the possible effects on the embryo and fetus of alcohol, illegal and over-the counter drugs, chemicals, and diseases, including AIDS.

* discuss the issues surrounding maternal age, maternal nutrition, emotional stress, and the role of the father during pregnancy.

* describe the opportunities and risks associated with new reproductive technologies.

* describe steps that can be taken to minimize the possibility of birth defects.

* describe the characteristics of the three stages of birth.

* define what is meant by a Cesarean birth, and discuss the long-term consequences of such a delivery.

* analyze the research concerning the short- and long-term effects of obstetrical medication.

* discuss different methods of giving birth, including the Lamaze and Leboyer approaches.

* discuss such birth complications as anoxia and premature delivery, and describe the special care premature infants require.

Study Questions

Consider these questions **before** you read the chapter:

1. In what sense is the prenatal stage the most important stage of life?

2. What are the key changes that occur during the
   a. germinal stage?
   b. embryonic stage?
   c. fetal stage?

3. What types of teratogens (agents that cause birth defects) are pregnant women commonly exposed to? During which periods of pregnancy are teratogens most dangerous?

4. What information should we give to pregnant women who smoke cigarettes or drink alcohol?

5. How might a pregnant woman's medical condition affect her pregnancy?

6. Why are so many children still being born with birth defects?

7. Why must couples get blood tests before they marry?

8. What is the relationship between each of the following and the health of the fetus?
   a. age of the mother
   b. the mother's nutritional status
   c. the emotional stress of the pregnant woman
   d. paternal drug use

9. How might a father's conflicting feelings about his wife's pregnancy affect the marital relationship?

10. Compare a traditional hospital delivery to the alternatives now available to prospective parents.

11. Describe how anoxia and premature delivery increase the risk of birth defects and what can be done to prevent them.

Study Questions Review

After you have studied Chapter Four, fill in this section.

1. In what sense is the prenatal stage the most important stage of life?

_____

_____

_____

_____

_____

_____

_____

2. What are the key changes that occur during the
   a. germinal stage?
   b. embryonic stage?
   c. fetal stage?

_____

_____

_____

_____

_____

_____

_____

_____

_____

3. What types of teratogens (agents that cause birth defects) are pregnant women commonly exposed to? During which periods of pregnancy are teratogens most dangerous?

_____

_____

_____

_____

_____

_____

_____

_____

_____

4. What information should we give to pregnant women who smoke cigarettes or drink alcohol?

_____

_____

_____

_____

_____

5. How might a pregnant woman's medical condition affect her pregnancy?

_____

_____

_____

_____

_____

6. Why are so many children still being born with birth defects?

_____

_____

_____

_____

_____

7. Why must couples get blood tests before they marry?

_____

_____

_____

_____

_____

8. What is the relationship between each of the following and the health of the fetus?
   a. age of the mother
   b. the mother's nutritional status
   c. the emotional stress of the pregnant woman
   d. paternal drug use

_____

_____

_____

_____

_____

_____

_____

_____

_____

9. How might a father's conflicting feelings about his wife's pregnancy affect the marital relationship?

_____

_____

_____

_____

_____

_____

_____

10. Compare the traditional hospital delivery to the alternatives now available to prospective parents.

_____

_____

_____

_____

_____

_____

11. Describe how anoxia and premature delivery increase the risk of birth defects and what can be done to prevent them.

_____

_____

_____

_____

_____

_____

_____

_____

_____

_____

_____

_____

Important Terms and Concepts

Match the following terms to their definitions below:

A. Fetal stage __
B. Labor __
C. APGAR __
D. Rubella __
E. Zygote __
F. Amniocentesis __
G. Transition __
H. Rh factor __
I. Blastocyst __
J. Crowning __
K. Expulsion __
L. Germinal stage __
M. Teratogen __
N. Prematurity __

O. Lamaze delivery __
P. Implantation __
Q. Critical period __
R. Chorionic villus sampling __
S. Fetal alcohol syndrome __
T. Embryonic stage __
U. Leboyer method __
V. Delivery of the placenta __
W. Sonogram __
X. Cesarean section __

Definitions

1. A fertilized egg

2. The earliest stage of prenatal development, lasting from conception to about two weeks

3. The stage of development in which the organism consists of layers of cells around a central cavity forming a hollow sphere

4. The process by which the fertilized egg burrows into the lining of the mother's uterus and obtains nourishment from her system

5. The stage of prenatal development, from about two weeks to about eight weeks, when bone cells begin to replace cartilage

6. The stage of prenatal development beginning at about eight weeks until birth

7. Any agent that can cause a birth defect

8. The period during which a particular event has its greatest impact

9. Retardation, growth defects, and other abnormalities of the infant associated with maternal alcohol consumption during pregnancy

10. A particular red-blood-cell antigen often found in humans

11. A procedure in which fluid is taken from a pregnant woman's uterus to check fetal cells for genetic and chromosomal abnormalities

12. A diagnostic procedure in which cells are taken from the chorion during the eighth to twelfth weeks of pregnancy and checked for abnormalities

13. The general process of expelling the fetus from the womb

14. A period late in labor in which the contractions become more difficult

15. The second stage of birth, involving actual delivery of the fetus

16. The point in labor at which the baby's head appears

17. The third and last stage of birth, in which the placenta is delivered

18. Approach to birth in which women are taught specific techniques for relaxing so that they need not depend on medication

19. A method of childbirth that attempts to minimize the discomfort of the newborn

20. A disease responsible for many cases of birth defects

21. Infants weighing less than 5 1/2 pounds or born less than thirty-seven weeks after conception

22. A relatively simple system of evaluating the newborn that gives a gross measure of infant survivability

23. An image of the developing organism taken through the use of sound waves

24. The birth procedure by which the fetus is surgically delivered through the abdominal wall and uterus

Answers

Self-test: Multiple Choice

1. The blastocyst is
a. an unfertilized egg.
b. a hollow ball of cells.
c. the lining of the placenta.
d. part of the uterus.

2. The placenta
a. delivers nutrients.
b. removes waste.
c. helps combat infection.
d. all of the above.

3. The first organ to function in the embryo is the
a. heart.
b. stomach.
c. brain.
d. liver.

4. The age of viability of the fetus is considered to be
a. 3 months.
b. 5 months.
c. 7 months.
d. 9 months.

5. The average normal male newborn weighs about
a. 5 1/2 pounds.
b. 7 1/2 pounds.
c. 9 pounds.
d. 12 pounds.

6. Which one of the following is least likely to cause harm to the fetus?
a. contraceptive pills
b. antibiotics
c. aspirin
d. strawberries

7. About what percentage of pregnant women smoke?
a. 11
b. 17
c. 27
d. 40

8. Maternal smoking increases the chances of
a. spontaneous abortion
b. fetal death
c. birth complications
d. all of the above

9. The effects of diseases like rubella on the fetus are greatest during
a. the first trimester.
b. the second trimester.
c. the third trimester.
d. the entire pregnancy.

10. As labor progresses
a. contractions get shorter.
b. contractions get weaker.
c. contractions occur more frequently.
d. all of the above.

11. A gentle delivery of newborns characterizes
a. rooming in.
b. LeBoyer.
c. Lamaze.
d. intensive care.

12. A premature infant weighs less than
a. 3 1/2 pounds.
b. 5 1/2 pounds.
c. 7 1/2 pounds.
d. 8 pounds.

13. Children born with fetal alcohol syndrome
a. eventually recover fully from its effects.
b. are likely to be of normal intelligence.
c. show serious long term effects of exposure to alcohol.
d. look just like normal children.

14. Using sound waves to produce a picture of the fetus is called
a. amniocentesis
b. chorionic villus sampling
c. a sonogram
d. dilation

Self-test: True-False
_1. Only one sperm can penetrate the outer membrane of the egg

_2. Fraternal twins come from the same egg

_3. The embryonic stage is the second of three stages of prenatal development

_4. There is no exchange of blood between the mother's circulatory system and that of the fetus

_5. Thumb-sucking and crying can occur in a five-month-old fetus

_6. The average female infant weights slightly more than the male

_7. The placental barrier protects the fetus from harmful chemicals the mother might ingest

_8. Most drugs have been shown to be safe for pregnant women

_9. The fetus has priority over the mother in getting its nutrients first

_10. A woman with a poor nutritional history can compensate for it by eating well while she is pregnant

_11. The more stress a pregnant woman is under, the greater the risk of birth complications

_12. Labor tends to become longer with each pregnancy

_13. Alcohol consumption by pregnant women is fairly common

_14. Caffeine and aspirin have been shown to be safe for pregnant women if taken during the last trimester

_15. Infants can contract venereal disease during their delivery

Answers

Multiple Choice

1. B	8. D
2. D	9. A
3. A	10. C
4. C	11. B
5. B	12. B
6. D	13. C
7. B	14. C

True-False

1. T	9. F
2. F	10. F
3. T	11. T
4. T	12. F
5. T	13. T
6. F	14. F
7. F	15. T
8. F	

Challenge Questions

1. At what point is the genetic endowment of the person-to-be set? What implications does this have for the validity of astrology, which claims that it is the position of the stars and planets at the moment of birth that determines personality?

_____

_____

_____

_____

_____

_____

_____

_____

2. What factors might determine the viability of the fetus at seven months?

_____

_____

_____

_____

_____

_____
_____

3. What precautions can a woman take to protect her fetus both before she is pregnant and while she is pregnant?

_____
_____
_____
_____
_____
_____

4. There are hundreds of thousands of births each year in the U.S. to unwed adolescents. Describe why the infants born to these young girls are at higher risk, prenatally and after birth. Can society prevent these problems before they occur?

_____
_____
_____
_____
_____
_____
_____
_____
_____
_____
_____

5. If you were about to become a proud parent, what choices might you make about the following (justify your choices)?:

a. use of anesthetics during delivery _____
_____
_____
_____
_____
_____

b. type of delivery _____
_____
_____

_____

_____

_____

_____

_____

c. rooming in _____

_____

_____

_____

_____

_____

Chapter Activities

1. Interview two pairs of parents about their pregnancy and birth experiences. What do they remember as the significant events in the total experience? Were there any problems prenatally, or during the birth itself? What type of delivery did they choose? Inquire about maternal stress, medication, and seeing and holding the newborn. Compare the results for the two couples.

2. Braun's (1996) **InfoTrac** article, New experiments underscore warnings on maternal drinking (In *Science, 273,* p. 738 (2)) reports that, despite warnings about alcohol as a prenatal risk factor, 20% of pregnant women drink. How can we make sense of this finding? Vogel's (1997) **InfoTrac** article, Cocaine wreaks subtle damage on developing brains (In *Science, 278,* p. 38 (2)) makes similar points regarding the effects of cocaine on the fetus. What can we do to convince expectant parents that exposing the fetus to alcohol and other drugs can have life long effects on the individual and family? In terms of intervention programs, what has been tried? What works, and what doesn't seem to work?

Physical Development *in* Infancy *and* Toddlerhood

Chapter Objectives

After studying Chapter Five of the text, you should be able to

* describe the appearance of a typical neonate and its visual abilities and preferences.

* describe the infant's sensory abilities in the areas of hearing, smell, taste, pressure, and pain.

* describe the infant's sleep-waking cycle and explain why the concept of state is important to understanding infant behavior.

* distinguish between different types of infant cries, and discuss the research on how parents can best respond to infant crying.

* interpret the research evidence concerning infants' ability to learn through conditioning and imitation.

* identify various neonatal reflexes such as the sucking, rooting, Babinsky, Moro, and grasping reflexes.

* discuss how the maturation of the brain affects infant abilities and behavior.

* describe how brain development is affected by experience.

* discuss the steps that parents can take to minimize the possibility of childhood diseases.

* list the risk factors that predict Sudden Infant Death Syndrome (SIDS).

* describe the principles of growth and development, including canalization and the cephalocaudal, proximodistal, and mass to specific principles.

* describe the biological and environmental factors that affect the development of motor skills.

* compare the social development of toddlers to that of infants.

* discuss the advantages and disadvantages of both breast-feeding and bottle-feeding.

* identify gender differences that can be observed in young children, and discuss the ways parents typically treat their sons and daughters differently.

* evaluate our current understanding of toilet training.

* describe the types of childhood problems that respond to early intervention efforts.

Study Questions

Consider these questions **before** you read the chapter:

1. Explain the quote, "infants are born well prepared for survival."

2. For the following, what abilities exist at birth and what abilities develop over time?
   a. visual acuity
   b. visual preferences
   c. color vision
   d. spatial and depth perception
   e. visual tracking
   f. hearing
   g. smell
   h. taste
   i. pressure and pain

3. What remarkable changes in sleep and dreaming occur during infancy?

4. What types of infant cries have been identified, and how can parents best respond to crying infants?

5. How do infants learn? Describe their capabilities regarding
   a. operant conditioning.
   b. imitation.

6. Select five reflexes present in the newborn and describe how they are adaptive (that is, how they promote survival)

7. What dramatic changes occur in an infant's brain between birth and six months of age?

8. Describe the role of each of the following in a child's motor development:
   a. heredity and maturation
   b. culture
   c. practice and stimulation

9. Why do many psychologists object to the concept of "the terrible twos"?

10. How is a toddler more competent than an infant?

11. What is the profile of a child considered at risk for Sudden Infant Death Syndrome?

12. What considerations should parents take into account regarding feeding their infants with breast or bottle? What is in the child's best interests? What about the mother's convenience?

13. How do parents view and raise their sons differently than how they view and raise their daughters?

14. How can parents facilitate the toilet training of their toddlers?

15. What can parents do when their toddlers show delayed development?

Study Questions Review

After you have studied Chapter Five, fill in this section.

1. Explain the statement, "infants are born well prepared for survival."

_____

_____

_____

_____

_____

_____

_____

_____

_____

2. For each of the following, describe what abilities exist at birth and what abilities develop over time:
   a. visual acuity
   b. visual preferences
   c. color vision
   d. spatial and depth perception
   e. visual tracking
   f. hearing
   g. smell
   h. taste
   i. pressure and pain

   _____
   _____
   _____
   _____
   _____
   _____
   _____
   _____
   _____
   _____
   _____
   _____

3. What remarkable changes in sleep and dreaming occur during infancy?

   _____
   _____
   _____
   _____
   _____
   _____
   _____
   _____

4. What types of infant cries have been identified, and how can parents best respond to crying infants?

   _____
   _____
   _____
   _____

_____
_____
_____
_____
_____
_____

5. How do infants learn? Describe the capabilities regarding
   a. operant conditioning.
   b. imitation.

_____
_____
_____
_____
_____
_____
_____
_____
_____
_____

6. Select five reflexes present in the newborn and describe how they are adaptive (that is, how they promote survival)

_____
_____
_____
_____
_____
_____
_____
_____
_____

7. What dramatic changes occur in an infant's brain between birth and six months of age?

_____
_____
_____
_____
_____
_____
_____

8. Describe the role of each of the following in a child's motor development:
   a. heredity and maturation
   b. culture
   c. practice and stimulation

_____
_____
_____
_____
_____
_____
_____
_____
_____
_____
_____
_____

9. Why do psychologists object to the concept of "the terrible twos"?

_____
_____
_____
_____
_____
_____
_____
_____

10. How is a toddler more competent than an infant?

_____
_____
_____
_____
_____
_____
_____
_____

11. What is the profile of a child considered at risk for Sudden Infant Death Syndrome?

_____

_____

_____

_____

_____

_____

_____

_____

_____

12. What considerations should parents take into account regarding feeding their infants with breast or bottle? What is in the child's best interests? What about the mother's convenience?

_____

_____

_____

_____

_____

_____

_____

_____

_____

13. How do parents view and raise their sons differently than how they view and raise their daughters?

_____

_____

_____

_____

_____

_____

_____

_____

14. How can parents facilitate the toilet training of their toddlers?

_____

_____

_____

_____

_____
_____
_____

15. What can parents do when their toddlers show delayed development?

_____
_____
_____
_____
_____
_____
_____

Important Terms and Concepts

Match each term to its definition below:

A. Toddler __
B. Reflex __
C. Canalization __
D. Mass to specific principle __
E. Rooting reflex __
F. Neonate __
G. Visual cliff __
H. Autonomy versus shame and doubt __
I. Sudden infant death syndrome __
J. Lanugo __
K. Habituation __

L. Dynamic Systems Theory __
M. Early intervention programs __
N. Fontanels __
O. Grasping reflex __
P. Cephalocaudal principle __
Q. Moro reflex __
R. Vernix Caseosa __
S. Sucking reflex __
T. Proximodistal principle __
U. Babinski reflex __
V. Trust versus mistrust

Definitions

1. The scientific term for a newborn infant

2. The fine hair that covers a newborn infant

3. A thick liquid that protects the skin of the fetus

4. The soft spots on the top of a baby's head

5. A device used to measure depth perception in infants

6. The process by which organisms spend less and less time attending to familiar stimuli

7. A relatively simple automatic reaction to a particular stimulus

8. A reflex found in young infants, in which they automatically suck when something is placed in their mouths

9. The reflex in young infants in which a stroke on the cheek causes them to turn in the direction of the stimulus

10. A reflex in which a stroke on the palm causes the infant to make a fist

11. The reflex in which stroking the soles of the feet results in the toes fanning out

12. A startle reflex to a loud noise or sudden change in position

13. The self-correcting process in which the child catches up in growth despite a moderate amount of stress or illness

14. A theory of motor development emphasizing the interaction between the organism and the environment

15. The growth principle stating that growth proceeds from the head downward to the trunk and feet

16. The growth principle stating that development occurs from the midline of the body toward the extremities

17. A principle of muscular development stating that control of the mass or large muscles precedes control of the fine muscles

18. The diagnosis given to young infants whose cause of death cannot be determined

19. A term designating the child between the ages of 1 and 3 years of age

20. Systematic efforts to assist infants and toddlers with developmental problems and their families

21. According to Erikson, the developmental crisis that occurs during the toddler stage

22. According to Erikson, the developmental crisis that occurs during infancy

Answers

A. 19	B. 7	C. 13
D. 17	E. 9	F. 1
G. 5	H. 21	I. 18
J. 2	K. 6	L. 14
M. 20	N. 4	O. 10
P. 15	Q. 12	R. 3
S. 8	T. 16	U. 11
V. 22		

Self-test: Multiple Choice

1. The thick secretion covering fetal skin is called
a. lanugo.
b. vernix caseosa.
c. kwashiokor.
d. marasmus.

2. The infant's visual acuity at birth is approximately
a. 20:20.
b. 20:50.
c. 20:100.
d. 20:200.

3. The young infant seems to have a visual preference for
a. complex stimuli.
b. human faces.
c. patterns.
d. all of the above.

4. In general, the perceptual abilities of the young infant
a. are absent.
b. are fully developed.
c. are difficult to study.
d. develop rapidly.

5. The least-developed perceptual ability in the newborn is
a. smell.
b. taste.
c. visual focusing.
d. touch.

6. About what percentage of the infant's sleep is spent in REM?
a. 30
b. 50
c. 65
d. 80

7. Infants spend most of their time
a. asleep.
b. crying.
c. playing.
d. studying.

8. Regarding the classical conditioning of infants, most studies
a. indicate strong conditioning.
b. indicate weak conditioning.
c. are mixed.
d. cannot be interpreted.

9. A simple form of learning that indicates an infant's ability to detect slight differences between stimuli is called
a. conditioning.
b. habituation.
c. adaptation.
d. reinforcement.

10. Reflexes are
a. learned.
b. innate.
c. not present in newborns.
d. complex responses to complex stimuli.

11. Victims of SIDS tend to be between the ages of
a. 1 to 2 months.
b. 2 to 4 months.
c. 4 to 6 months.
d. over 6 months.

12. The switch from lower brain to cortical control occurs by the age of
a. 3 months.
b. 6 months.
c. 1 year.
d. puberty.

13. Growth that occurs in spurts rather than gradually is called
a. dynamic
b. proximodistal
c. neonatal
d. saltatory

14. It is easiest to toilet train an infant when the infant is
a. a boy.
b. 18 months old.
c. active.
d. ready.

15. Turning their cheeks in the direction of a facial stroke is referred to as the --- reflex.
a. Moro
b. Babinski
c. feeding
d. rooting

Self-test: True-False

_1. At birth, infants are essentially blind.

_2. Young infants do show visual preferences.

_3. Newborns can see color.

_4. Infants cannot see as well as adults until they are about one year old.

_5. Infants can hear from the moment of birth.

_6. Newborns are attracted to unpleasant odors.

_7. Young infants will drink more water if there is sugar in it.

_8. Infants are relatively insensitive to pain.

_9. Infants appear to dream less than older children or adults.

_10. Infant behavior changes according to the particular state the infant is in.

_11. The infant's earliest cries are attempts to communicate.

_12. Picking up a crying infant will "spoil" the infant.

_13. Young infants can easily be operantly conditioned.

_14. Imitative responses can occur within hours of birth.

_15. Most brain areas are well-developed at birth.

_16. Male and female infants are far more alike than different.

Answers

Multiple Choice

1. B	9. B
2. D	10. B
3. D	11. B
4. D	12. B
5. C	13. D
6. B	14. D
7. A	15. D
8. C	

True-False

1. F	9. F
2. T	10. T
3. T	11. F
4. F	12. F
5. T	13. T
6. F	14. T
7. T	15. F
8. F	16. T

Challenge Questions

1. How are the perceptual abilities and the reflexes of the newborn adaptive, given the nature of the environment into which human infants are born?

_____
_____
_____
_____
_____
_____
_____

2. Why are more and more educated women choosing to breast-feed rather than bottle-feed their infants? Why is the trend in the Third World in the opposite direction?

_____

_____

_____

_____

_____

_____

_____

_____

_____

_____

3. What is it about toddlers' new abilities that might give them the "terrible two's" reputation?

_____

_____

_____

_____

_____

_____

_____

_____

Chapter Activities

1. With the permission of the parent, observe the behavior of a newborn and report your findings. What reflexes can you elicit? What types of body and facial movements does the infant make? What types of sounds can you identify? Is the infant responsive to social stimuli, such as smiles and speech sounds?

2. Based on Bracey's (1996) **InfoTrac** article, The impact of early intervention (In *Phi Delta Kappan, 77,* p. 510 (2)), address the following questions:
1. What is the logic of early intervention programs?
2. What type of population typically is selected for such programs?
3. What was the nature of the intervention in this project?
4. How was success measured?
5. What were the main findings of this project?
6. Which factors seem to make the most difference?
7. What are the main limitations of the project? How did they affect the interpretation of the data?

Cognitive *and* Linguistic Development *in* Infancy *and* Toddlerhood

Chapter Objectives

After studying Chapter Six of the text, you should be able to

* describe Piaget's sensorimotor stage and its six substages.

* define what is meant by deferred imitation and object permanence and describe how they develop.

* evaluate Piaget's theory in the light of research studies that have tested its predictions.

* describe the development of recall and recognition memory in infants.

* review attempts by developmental psychologists to measure and predict children's intellectual abilities.

* discuss the relationship between an infant's socioeconomic status, its home environment, and its cognitive development.

* describe parental activities that encourage cognitive growth in children.

* list the key ingredients of effective parent training programs.

* discuss the pros and cons of "accelerating" children's cognitive development.

* distinguish between language and communication.

* list and define the subsystems of language.

* describe the sequence of language development from prelanguage communication through adolescence.

* describe the role of reinforcement and imitation in language learning.

* describe the errors that young children make in their early speech and what these errors tell us about their understanding of language rules.

* evaluate the nativist and cognitive theories of language acquisition.

* describe the functions of social interaction and verbal exchanges in language development.

* describe what parents can do to encourage language development in their children.

* discuss the issue surrounding children's use of Black English in schools.

* discuss the best way of educating bilingual children.

Study Questions

Consider these questions **before** you read the chapter:

1. In what sense are infants intelligent?

2. What role do the following play in Piaget's theory of cognitive development?
   a. repeated actions
   b. mental representations of the world
   c. awareness of being separate from the rest of the world
   d. the concept of stages of cognitive development

3. Briefly describe the main achievement of each of the six substages of cognitive development, according to Piaget.

4. Describe how object permanence sets the stage for further gains in cognitive development.

5. What criticisms have been expressed about Piaget's methods and assumptions?

6. Distinguish between:
   a. recognition memory.
   b. recall.

7. Why might adults have difficulty remembering events from early childhood?

8. Describe the types of instruments used to assess the intelligence of preverbal children. How useful are these devices?

9. What is the relationship between each of the following and children's cognitive growth?
   a. family socioeconomic level
   b. home environment
   c. unrealistic parental expectations

10. How can the home environment be improved to better cultivate cognitive growth?

11. How do infants communicate before they have learned actual words?

12. What prelinguistic abilities emerge before infants begin to speak?

13. How do expressive children use speech differently from referential children? How does their parents' speech differ?

14. Describe the transition from one-word speech to telegraphic speech to the use of spoken sentences

15. What is the main difference between the speech of infants and that of toddlers?

16. What evidence supports the nativist model of language acquisition? What evidence contradicts it?

17. What evidence supports the learning model? What limitations do we find in the learning model?

18. How do parents adjust their speech to make it more comprehensible to young children?

19. Are children advantaged or disadvantaged by being bilingual?

20. In what ways can parents encourage the acquisition of language in their children?

Study Questions Review

After you have studied Chapter Six, fill in this section.

1. In what sense are infants intelligent?

_____

_____

_____

_____

2. What role do the following play in Piaget's theory of cognitive development?
   a. repeated actions
   b. mental representations of the world
   c. awareness of being separate from the rest of the world
   d. the concept of stages of cognitive development

_____

_____

_____

_____

_____

_____

_____

_____

_____

3. Briefly describe the main achievement of each of the six substages of cognitive development, according to Piaget.

_____

_____

_____

_____

_____

_____

_____

_____

_____

4. Describe how object permanence sets the stage for further gains in cognitive development.

_____

_____

_____

_____

_____

5. What criticisms have been expressed about Piaget's methods and assumptions?

_____

_____

_____

_____

_____

_____

_____

_____

_____

_____

6. Distinguish between:
   a. recognition memory.
   b. recall.

_____

_____

_____

_____

_____

7. Why might adults have difficulty remembering events from early childhood?

_____

_____

_____

_____

8. Describe the types of instruments used to assess the intelligence of preverbal children. How useful are these devices?

_____

_____

_____

_____

_____

_____

_____
_____
_____
_____

9. What is the relationship between each of the following and children's cognitive growth?
   a. family socioeconomic level
   b. home environment
   c. unrealistic parental expectations

_____
_____
_____
_____
_____
_____
_____
_____
_____

10. How can the home environment be improved to better cultivate cognitive growth?

_____
_____
_____
_____
_____
_____
_____
_____
_____
_____
_____

11. How do infants communicate before they have learned actual words?

_____
_____
_____
_____

12. What prelinguistic abilities emerge before infants begin to speak?

_____
_____
_____
_____
_____

13. How do expressive children use speech differently from referential children? How does their parents' speech differ?

_____
_____
_____
_____
_____
_____
_____
_____
_____
_____

14. Describe the transition from one-word speech to telegraphic speech to the use of spoken sentences

_____
_____
_____
_____
_____
_____
_____
_____
_____
_____

15. What is the main difference between the speech of infants and that of toddlers?

_____
_____
_____
_____
_____

16. What evidence supports the nativist model of language acquisition? What evidence contradicts it?

_____
_____
_____
_____
_____
_____
_____
_____
_____

17. What evidence supports the learning model? What limitations do we find in the learning model?

_____
_____
_____
_____
_____
_____
_____
_____
_____

18. How do parents adjust their speech to make it more comprehensible to young children?

_____
_____
_____
_____
_____
_____
_____
_____
_____

19. Are children advantaged or disadvantaged by being bilingual? Explain.

_____
_____
_____
_____
_____

20. In what ways can parents encourage the acquisition of language in their children?

_____
_____
_____
_____
_____
_____
_____
_____
_____

Important Terms and Concepts

I. Cognitive Development

     Match the term to its definition below:

A. Recall __
B. Tertiary circular reaction __
C. Object permanence __
D. Recognition __
E. Infantile amnesia __
F. Primary circular reaction __
G. Deferred imitation __
H. Secondary circular reaction __

Definitions

1. In Piaget's model, actions that are repeated over and over again by infants

2. In Piaget's model, repetitive actions that are intended to create some environmental reaction

3. Repetitive actions with some variations each time

4. The ability to observe an act and imitate it at a later time

5. The understanding that an object exists even when it is out of one's visual field

6. A way of testing retention in which the subject is required to choose the correct answer from a group of choices

7. A way of testing retention in which the subject must produce the correct response given very limited cues

8. The inability of adults to recall events that occur during infancy and toddlerhood

Answers

A. 7
B. 3
C. 5
D. 6
E. 8
F. 1
G. 4
H. 2

II. Language Acquisition

Match the term to its definition below:

A. Syntax __   M. Telegraphic speech __
B. Grammar __   N. Phonology __
C. Broca's area __   O. Semantics __
D. Comprehension __   P. Wernicke's area __
E. Holophrase __   Q. Nativist explanation __
F. Babbling __   R. Referential children __
G. Communication __   S. Pragmatics __
H. Overgeneralization __   T. Underextension __
I. Fine-tuning theory __   U. Morphology __
J. Language __   V. Morpheme __
K. Expressive children __   W. Cooing __
L. Production __   X. Representation

Definitions

1. The process of sharing information

2. Use of arbitrary symbols with agreed upon meaning

3. The study of the sounds of language, the rules for combining them to make words and stress and intonation patterns

4. The study of the patterns of word formation in a particular language

5. The smallest unit of meaning in a language

6. The rules for combining words to make sentences

7. The study of the meaning of words

8. The total linguistic knowledge of phonology, morphology, syntax, and semantics

9. The study of how people use language in various contexts

10. Vowel and consonant sounds strung together and often repeated by infants

11. Children who use words involved in social interactions

12. Children whose early language is used to name objects

13. One word used to stand for an entire thought or sentence

14. Sentences in which only the basic words necessary to communicate meaning are used with helping words left out

15. A type of error in which children apply a term more broadly than it should be

16. The use of a word in a more narrow context than proper

17. The ability to verbalize language

18. The ability to understand language

19. The theory that human beings are preprogrammed to learn language

20. An area in the brain responsible for producing speech

21. An area in the brain responsible for comprehending speech

22. A theory that parents tune their language to a child's linguistic ability

23. Verbal production of single-syllable sounds

24. The ability to go beyond physical actions and to use symbols to mentally portray events and feelings

Answers

A. 6	B. 8	C. 20
D. 18	E. 13	F. 10
G. 1	H. 15	I. 22
J. 2	K. 11	L. 17
M. 14	N. 3	O. 7
P. 21	Q. 19	R. 12
S. 9	T. 16	U. 4
V. 5	W. 23	X. 24

Self-test: Multiple Choice

1. Cognitive development generally refers to how children
a. come to make sense of their experiences.
b. learn how to cope with stressful life experiences.
c. fulfill their genetic potential to achieve.
d. learn to communicate with others.

2. Primary circular reactions
a. occur during the first month of infancy.
b. are repeated activities focusing on the infant's body.
c. are repeated actions focusing on the external environment.
d. reveal the infant's intentions.

3. Children are capable of deferred imitation
a. at birth.
b. by the age of one year.
c. by the age of two years.
d. only if they receive specific training.

4. Naming the presidents of the United States is an example of
a. recall memory.
b. recognition memory.
c. concept formation.
d. habituation.

5. The Bayley scales of infant development
a. are based on interviews with parents.
b. are based on observations of children's growth patterns.
c. can be administered to newborns.
d. do not predict later intellectual functioning for normal infants.

6. One of the most promising ways of improving children's intellectual abilities is
a. free school lunch programs.
b. mass immunizations.
c. better educational television programming.
d. training parents to improve their children's home environments.

7. Cognitive development
a. is controlled by heredity and maturation.
b. is controlled by environmental stimulation.
c. reflects a complex interaction between maturation and learning.
d. cannot be accelerated by enrichment programs.

8. Mothers who are poor tend not to
a. have good recognition memory
b. talk very much to their children.
c. love their children as much as middle class parents.
d. value achievement.

9. Parents can learn helpful parenting skills through
a. demonstration.
b. watching films.
c. home visits by professionals.
d. all of the above

10. The optimal way of encouraging children's cognitive growth is
a. providing brief, interesting interactions throughout the day.
b. buying them expensive toys
c. teaching them to read before they start school.
d. providing massive amounts of stimulation.

11. Language
a. is the process of sharing information.
b. requires vocalizations.
c. does not emerge until toddlerhood.
d. involves the use of symbols.

12. Cooing consists of
a. consonant sounds.
b. vowel sounds.
c. cries of distress.
d. lip movements in deaf children.

13. A single word that stands for a complete idea is called
a. babbling.
b. a pivot word.
c. holophrastic speech.
d. prelinguistic.

14. A child's use of the word "foots" exemplifies
a. overextension.
b. overgeneralization.
c. a syntax error.
d. proto-conversation.

15. The leading advocate of nativist language theory is
a. Skinner.
b. Piaget.
c. Chomsky.
d. Broca.

16. Which one of the following does **not** indicate motherese?
a. shorter sentences
b. lower pitch
c. asking questions
d. using simple words

17. To be considered a child's first word, the word must
a. resemble a real word.
b. be used consistently.
c. both a. and b. are correct.
d. neither a. nor b. is correct.

18. Eighteen month olds speak about __ words
a. 5
b. 12
c. 18
d. 50

19. "Mommy go store" exemplifies what type of speech?
a. holophrastic
b. telegraphic
c. French
d. bilingual

20. Skinner's approach to language acquisition would emphasize the role of
a. biology.
b. reinforcement.
c. language-acquisition devices.
d. Broca's area.

21. Parents are likely to reinforce their children's utterances on the basis of
a. the correctness of the grammar.
b. the truthfulness of the statement.
c. the parent's opinion about the matter.
d. the complexity of the utterance.

Self-test: True-False

__1. Piaget believed that infants occasionally skip substages in the sensorimotor stage.

__2. All healthy children enter and leave a substage at the same age.

__3. Research in cognitive development has generally supported Piaget's theory.

__4. Recall is usually harder than recognition.

__5. A child's intelligence can be predicted from his or her performance on infant I.Q. tests.

__6. Mothers from lower socioeconomic levels speak to their children more than middle class mothers speak to theirs.

__7. Early home environment is a good predictor of I.Q. at age three.

__8. Parents who most need parent training are usually the first ones to sign up for parent training programs.

__9. It is pointless to speak or read to young children who do not yet understand words.

__10. Overstimulating children has proven to be a more serious problems than understimulating them.

__11. Deferred imitation is a good sign that an infant is capable of symbolic representation.

__12. Developmental psychologists now believe that they have a good understanding of what young children are capable of knowing and doing.

__13. Communication does not require language.

__14. Language production precedes language comprehension.

__15. "Syntax" refers to the rules for combining words to make sentences.

__16. Bilingual children are at a disadvantage in school.

__17. Babbling involves both vowel and consonant sounds that are strung together and repeated.

__18. Early words are generally learned through imitation.

__19. Language-acquisition devices have been found in the human brain.

_20. Teenagers use words more abstractly than younger children.

_21. Very young children can generate, without effort, meaningful, grammatical sentences that they have never heard anyone speak before.

_22. It is not known whether giving children feedback about the correctness of their utterances helps them learn language.

_23. Reading to infants helps them learn about their parents' language.

Answers

Multiple Choice

1. A	6. D
2. B	7. C
3. C	8. B
4. A	9. D
5. D	10. A

11. D	17. C
12. A	18. C
13. C	19. B
14. B	20. B
15. C	21. B
16. B	

True-False

1. F	7. T
2. F	8. F
3. T	9. F
4. T	10. F
5. F	11. T
6. F	12. F

13. T	19. F
14. F	20. T
15. T	21. T
16. F	22. T
17. T	23. T
18. T	

Challenge Questions

1. Cognitive development encompasses how we come to make sense of our experiences. What role might cognitive development play in a child's family life?

_____

_____

_____

_____

_____

_____

2. Researchers in cognitive development study what infants know. What problems might these researchers encounter in answering this question. Can you explain why they sometimes overestimate what children know? (Hint- What role does children's language ability play in our interpretation of what they know?)

_____

_____

_____

_____

_____

_____

_____

_____

_____

3. What are your two earliest memories? How vivid are they? How confident are you about their validity, that is, that they really occurred? What was it about these early experiences that led to their retention?

_____

_____

_____

_____

_____

_____

_____

_____

4. One of the best predictors of a child's intellectual development is his or her mother's educational level. Why do you think this is true? What advantages might children whose mothers are more educated have?

_____

_____

_____
_____
_____
_____
_____
_____

5. Language is one of the clearest examples of an ability that separates humans from other species. What aspects of human speech appear to be biologically rooted? What aspects appear to be learned?

_____
_____
_____
_____
_____
_____
_____
_____
_____

6. Many parents read to their infants even though the infants do not understand a word they are hearing. How might these youngsters gain from exposure to spoken language? What other types of stimulation or enrichment experiences might encourage language acquisition?

_____
_____
_____
_____
_____
_____
_____
_____
_____
_____
_____
_____
_____

7. Explain what is meant by the statement, "Language ability is a fundamental skill."

_____
_____
_____
_____
_____

_____

_____

_____

_____

_____

_____

_____

_____

_____

_____

_____

Chapter Activities

1. Tape record the verbalizations of a preschool child for 15 minutes. Then, analyze the sounds according to words used, length of sentences, the complexity of the ideas expressed, the types of errors committed, and so on. Report your findings in terms of the material covered in Chapter Six.

2. Devise a brief intelligence test for children of a particular age and administer it to three young children. Construct verbal and nonverbal (performance) items that you believe will assess a child's abilities. Invent a way of scoring the test. In reporting your results, compare the three children's performances. (Assure parents that your test is simply an exercise and is not meant to provide a realistic assessment of their children's abilities.)

3. According to the **InfoTrac** study of Yoshinago-Itano et al. (1998), Language of early- and later-identified children with hearing loss (In *Pediatrics, 102,* p. 1161 (11)), how does hearing loss affect the development of language skills in children? Why is early diagnosis critical for normal language development?

Social *and* Personality Development *in* Infancy *and* Toddlerhood

Chapter Objectives

After studying Chapter Seven of the text, you should be able to:

* describe emotional reactions that are present at birth and those that emerge during the first several months after birth.

* distinguish between primary and secondary emotions.

* describe the cognitive abilities behind secondary emotions.

* explain the dynamics of social referencing.

* discuss the social nature of smiling during infancy.

* describe the origins of empathy and its role in close relationships.

* distinguish between attachment and attachment behavior.

* describe the three stages in children's reaction to prolonged separation.

* describe the effects of maternal deprivation and various interpretations of the effects of institutionalization.

* distinguish between secure attachment and three forms of insecure attachment.

* discuss the apparent causes of insecure attachment.

* describe the parenting styles that are associated with each form of attachment.

* analyze how maternal depression could affect infant attachment.

* describe the relationship between infant temperament and attachment.

* describe environmental factors that increase infants' fear of strangers and separation anxiety.

* distinguish between typical mother-infant and father-infant relationships.

* interpret the research concerning the effects of maternal employment on children's development.

* analyze the relationship between day care and attachment.

* list the characteristics of high quality day care.

Study Questions

Consider these questions **before** you read the chapter.

1. What role do emotions play in the strong bonds that develop between parents and children?

2. Distinguish between those elements of emotion that are innate, those that are learned, and those that are cognitive.

3. Describe how emotional and cognitive development are related during infancy, using fear of strangers and separation anxiety as examples.

4. Why does an infant's smile have such powerful effects on parental emotions and behavior?

5. How do infants use other people's facial expressions to guide their own emotional reactions?

6. In what sense are stranger anxiety and separation distress adaptive?

7. Why is secure attachment crucial for a child's emotional development?

8. What long-term effects might inadequate parenting, or institutionalization, have on infant development?

9. How do securely attached children behave differently from less securely attached children?

10. How involved is the traditional father in the raising of his children? How do father interactions with young children differ from mother interactions?

11. How can we distinguish high quality day care from low quality day care?

12. What has research revealed about the effects of maternal employment on young children's development?

Study Questions Review

After you have studied the chapter, fill in this section.

1. What role do emotions play in the strong bonds that develop between parents and children?

_____

_____

_____

_____

_____

_____

_____

_____

2. Distinguish between those elements of emotion that are innate, those that are learned, and those that are cognitive.

_____

_____

_____

_____

_____

_____

_____

_____

_____

_____

3. Describe how emotional and cognitive development are related during infancy, using fear of strangers and separation anxiety as examples.

_____

_____

_____

_____

_____

_____

_____

_____
_____
_____

4. Why does an infant's smile have such powerful effects on parental emotions and behavior?

_____
_____
_____
_____

5. How do infants use other people's facial expressions to guide their own emotional reactions?

_____
_____
_____
_____
_____
_____
_____
_____

6. In what sense are stranger anxiety and separation distress adaptive?

_____
_____
_____
_____
_____
_____

7. Why is secure attachment crucial for a child's emotional development?

_____
_____
_____
_____
_____
_____

8. What long-term effects might inadequate parenting, or institutionalization, have on infant development?

_____

_____

_____

_____

_____

_____

_____

_____

9. How do securely attached children behave differently from less securely attached children?

_____

_____

_____

_____

10. How involved is the traditional father in the raising of his children? How do father interactions with young children differ from mother interactions?

_____

_____

_____

_____

_____

_____

_____

_____

_____

11. How can we distinguish high quality day care from low quality day care?

_____

_____

_____

_____

_____

_____

12. What has research revealed about the effects of maternal employment on young children's development?

_____
_____
_____
_____
_____
_____
_____
_____
_____
_____

Important Terms and Concepts

Match the term to its definition below

A. Imprinting __   L. Anxious disorganized __
B. Hospitalism __   M. Secure attachment __
C. Contact comfort __   N. Differential emotions theory __
D. Strange situation __   O. Primary emotions __
E. Social referencing __   P. Secondary emotions __
F. Attachment __   Q. Empathy __
G. Synchrony __   R. Attachment behavior __
H. Separation anxiety __   S. Father __
I. anxious/avoidant attachment __
J. anxious/resistant attachment __
K. Fear of strangers __

Definitions

1. The phenomenon in which a person uses information received from others to appraise events and regulate behavior

2. A common phenomenon beginning in the second half of the first year, consisting of a fear response to unfamiliar people

3. A phenomenon in which young children show intense distress upon being separated from their caretakers

4. Emotions that require more sophisticated cognitive abilities

5. Reacting emotionally to other people's emotional displays

6. The male parent

7. A strong affectional tie between two people

8. Actions that keep children in the vicinity of caregivers

9. A condition found in children from substandard institutions, marked by emotional disturbances, failure to gain weight, and retardation

10. The need for physical touching and fondling

11. A type of attachment in which the child shows a variety of contradictory behaviors during the mother's reentrance after a brief separation

12. An experimental procedure used to measure attachment behaviors

13. A type of attachment in which the infant uses a caregiver as a secure base of operations

14. A type of attachment behavior in which a child avoids reestablishing contact with the mother as she reenters the room after a brief separation

15. A theory that young infants possess a limited number of emotions

16. Innate emotions that result from biological programming

17. A type of attachment behavior in which the child both seeks close contact and resists it during the mother's reentrance after a brief separation

18. The coordination between the infant and caregiver in which each responds to the subtle verbal and nonverbal cues of the other

19. An irreversible, rigid pattern of attachment

Answers

A. 19	B. 9	C. 10
D. 12	E. 1	F. 7
G. 18	H. 3	I. 14
J. 17	K. 2	L. 11
M. 13	N. 15	O. 16
P. 4	Q. 5	R. 8
S. 6		

Self-test: Multiple Choice

1. A social smile can be elicited in an infant three weeks after birth by
a. a high pitched human voice.
b. a smiling human face.
c. an unfamiliar person.
d. gentle rocking.

2. Infant emotions
a. facilitate behavior reactions to stimuli.
b. communicate the infant's state to others.
c. encourage caregivers to help the infant.
d. all of the above

3. Facial expressions accompanying emotions
a. vary according to particular cultures.
b. reflect learning more than heredity.
c. are virtually the same for all humans.
d. can be accurately interpreted by newborns.

4. The infant's tendency to use the facial expressions of others to appraise events and regulate behavior is called
a. synchrony.
b. imprinting.
c. hospitalism.
d. social referencing.

5. According to Bowlby, the first stage children go through in reaction to prolonged separation is
a. protest.
b. detachment.
c. despair.
d. denial.

6. Harlow's monkeys derived ___ from their terrycloth mothers
a. contact comfort
b. southern comfort
c. stimulus enrichment
d. anxious attachment

7. The strange situation procedure is used to test
a. cognitive development.
b. security of attachment.
c. the home environment.
d. degree of autonomy.

8. Wayne Dennis's study showed that children need at least a minimal amount of
a. food
b. love
c. stimulation
d. touch

9. Fathers participate more in child care when
a. mothers are employed full time.
b. there is more than one child.
c. mothers expect or demand it.
d. all of the above

10. The most common activity fathers engage in with their young children is
a. feeding.
b. play.
c. reading.
d. shopping.

11. Most mothers work because
a. they do not find satisfaction in child care.
b. their families require their income.
c. they do not like to be dependent on their husband's income.
d. it is a way of achieving personal fulfillment.

12. The effects of maternal employment on children are generally
a. positive.
b. negative.
c. positive or negative, depending upon many factors.
d. not understood.

13. Most infants in day care show
a. secure attachment.
b. insecure attachment.
c. signs of hospitalism.
d. delayed growth.

14. The child-caregiver relationship as affected by
a. the caregiver's emotional problems
b. the caregiver's attachment status
c. the caregiver's parenting style
d. all of the above

Self-test: True-False

_1. The infant's smile encourages the caregiver to interact more with the child.

_2. The expression of stranger anxiety in infants depends upon the specific circumstances.

_3. Infants tend to cry when they hear the cries of other infants.

_4. Separation anxiety peaks at about the age of two years.

_5. An infant's attachment to its mother is present at birth.

_6. The dominant emotion during the protest stage of prolonged separation is fear.

_7. Harlow found that the injurious consequences of a lack of mothering are permanent.

_8. Securely attached infants tend to be more enthusiastic and more persistent than children who are not securely attached.

_9. Three-week old infants smile both to social and nonsocial stimuli.

_10. Mothers who work get significant help from their husbands in child care.

_11. Infants tend to choose mothers over fathers when they are hungry, wet, or distressed.

_12. Fathers can be excellent caregivers, when they want to be.

_13. Children of working mothers are at higher risk for juvenile delinquency and personality disorders.

_14. Most children in day care are cared for in their own home or someone else's home.

Answers

Multiple Choice

1. A	8. C
2. D	9. D
3. C	10. B
4. D	11. B
5. A	12. C
6. A	13. A
7. B	14. D

True-False

1. T	8. T
2. T	9. T
3. T	10. F
4. F	11. T
5. F	12. T
6. F	13. F
7. F	14. T

Challenge Questions

1. Young children's emotional development seems to depend most on their interactions with their parents. What aspects of a parents' personality, moods, and emotionality might be particularly influential? What role might imitation play?

_____
_____
_____
_____
_____
_____
_____
_____

2. Although parents might complain about their infant's fear of strangers and separation fears, these fear reactions are adaptive (i.e., have survival value). Describe how.

_____
_____
_____
_____
_____
_____
_____

3. What would you do to reduce your child's separation distress

a. when leaving your child with a new babysitter? _____
_____
_____
_____
_____

b. on the first day of school? _____

_____

_____

_____

_____

_____

4. Harlow demonstrated his monkeys' need for contact comfort when they clung to soft cloth dolls. Can you describe behaviors you have observed in human infants that suggest a need for contact comfort?

_____

_____

_____

_____

_____

_____

_____

_____

_____

_____

5. What considerations would you have if you were looking for day care for your young child? What questions would you ask the director? What qualifications would you expect in the staff? What else would you look for regarding equipment, facilities, and safety?

_____

_____

_____

_____

_____

_____

_____

_____

_____

6. Should mothers of preschool children work or should they stay home with their children? (Is this a sexist question?). What is in the best interests of the child? What is in the best interests of the mother?

Chapter Activities

1. Interview two children and their parents about the children's fears. What are the children afraid of and why? How do they cope with their fears. How do parents react when their children are fearful? Report your findings.

2. Observe two infants (one at a time) while they are seated in a parent's lap. Notice how often the infants glance at their parents' faces. Do the infants' reactions coincide with parental facial expressions or tone of voice? What other forms of social referencing do you see? Report your findings.

3. The **InfoTrac** articles cited below address the topics of child care and infant attachment. Based on your reading of these articles and textbook chapter 7, describe how investigators define and study attachment. Does the child care system in the United States satisfy infants' attachment needs? What are the key components of high quality care programs? What do parents need to know to raise emotionally healthy children?

Cottle, M (1998). Who's watching the kids? *Washington Monthly, 30,* p. 16 (10).

Field, T. (1996). Attachment and separation in young children. *Annual Review of Psychology, 47,* p. 541 (21).

Lehman, E.B., Arnold, B.E., & Reeves, S.L. (1995). Attachment to blankets, teddy bears, and other nonsocial objects: A child's perspective. *Journal of Genetic Psychology, 156,* p. 443 (17).

Shaw, D.S. & Vondra, J.I. (1995). Infant attachment security and maternal predictors of early behavior problems: A longitudinal study of low-income families. *Journal of Abnormal Child Psychology, 23,* p. 335 (23).

Physical *and* Cognitive Development *in* Early Childhood

Chapter Objectives

After studying Chapter Eight of the text, you should be able to:

* describe the growth and motor development of preschool children.

* describe the developmental progressions shown in children's drawing and painting.

* discuss the issues surrounding preschoolers' dietary preferences and nutrition.

* cite common threats to children's health worldwide.

* describe changes in children's nervous system during the preschool years.

* summarize the advances and limitations in the reasoning of preschool children.

* describe advances in preschoolers' speech, including grammar, vocabulary, and conversation.

* identify challenges to and expansions of Piaget's theory and its current status.

* discuss the implications of the study of preschoolers' attentional and memory skills for their education.

* illustrate how children use schemata and scripts to guide their behavior.

* discuss how the home and family environment can affect the cognitive development of preschoolers.

* analyze the research concerning the effects of television advertising and programming on children's cognitive development.

* distinguish between the major types of nursery schools and interpret the research concerning the influence of preschool on children's cognitive development.

* discuss the goals and the effectiveness of Head Start programs.

* evaluate the changes in modern kindergarten classes.

Study Questions

Consider these questions **before** you read the chapter:

1. What significant changes in growth occur in early childhood?

2. How do preschoolers' emerging motor skills allow them greater independence?

3. How do we know that environment plays a role in determining handedness?

4. How is drawing a valuable childhood activity?

5. How might a preschooler's newfound motor abilities place him or her in jeopardy? What can parents do to protect their youngsters from danger in the home?

6. What can parents do to ensure that their children are eating properly?

7. What are the major threats to young children's health worldwide?

8. What changes in the brain appear to underlie preschoolers' cognitive advances?

9. What are the key cognitive advances during the preoperational stage? The key limitations, including egocentrism?

10. How do preschoolers benefit from self talk?

11. Distinguish between inductive, deductive, and transductive reasoning.

12. What role does training appear to play in a preschooler's ability to demonstrate conservation and classification?

13. What are the most frequent challenges to Piaget's view of preschool children?

14. How has recent research changed our view of young children's attention and memory?

15. What are the key issues surrounding children's television watching?

16. Do nursery school programs fulfill their objectives?

17. How successful have Head Start programs been in reducing the gap between disadvantaged and middle-class children?

18. How has kindergarten changed over the past decade? What is its primary function?

Study Questions Review

After you have studied Chapter Eight, fill in this section.

1. What significant changes in growth occur in early childhood?

_____
_____
_____
_____
_____
_____
_____
_____
_____
_____

2. How do preschoolers' emerging motor skills allow them greater independence?

_____
_____
_____
_____
_____

3. How do we know that environment plays a role in determining handedness?

_____
_____
_____
_____
_____
_____
_____
_____
_____

4. How is drawing a valuable childhood activity?

_____
_____
_____
_____
_____

5. How might a preschooler's newfound motor abilities place him or her in jeopardy? What can parents do to protect their youngsters from danger in the home?

_____
_____
_____
_____
_____
_____
_____
_____
_____

6. What can parents do to ensure that their children are eating properly?

_____
_____
_____
_____
_____

7. What are the major threats to young children's health worldwide?

_____
_____
_____
_____
_____
_____
_____
_____
_____
_____
_____
_____

8. What changes in the brain appear to underlie preschoolers' cognitive advances?

_____

_____

_____

_____

9. What are the key cognitive advances during the preoperational stage? The key limitations, including egocentrism?

_____

_____

_____

_____

_____

_____

_____

_____

_____

10. How do preschoolers benefit from self talk?

_____

_____

_____

_____

_____

11. Distinguish between inductive, deductive, and transductive reasoning.

_____

_____

_____

_____

_____

_____

_____

_____

12. What role does training appear to play in a preschooler's ability to demonstrate conservation and classification?

_____
_____
_____
_____
_____
_____
_____

13. What are the most frequent challenges to Piaget's view of preschool children?

_____
_____
_____
_____
_____
_____
_____
_____
_____

14. How has recent research changed our view of young children's attention and memory?

_____
_____
_____
_____
_____
_____
_____
_____
_____

15. What are the key issues surrounding children's television watching?

_____
_____
_____
_____
_____
_____
_____

16. Do most nursery school programs fulfill their objectives? Explain.

_____

_____

_____

_____

_____

_____

_____

17. How successful have Head Start programs been in reducing the gap between disadvantaged and middle-class children?

_____

_____

_____

_____

_____

_____

_____

18. How has kindergarten changed over the past decade? What is its primary function?

_____

_____

_____

_____

_____

_____

_____

_____

Important Terms and Concepts

Match the term to its definition below:

A. Centering __
B. Animism __
C. Metamemory __
D. Preoperational stage __
E. Seriation __
F. Transitive inferences __
G. Inductive reasoning __
H. Conservation __
I. Selective attention __
J. Deductive reasoning __

K. Project Head Start __
L. Artificialism __
M. Transductive reasoning __
N. Compensatory education __
O. Reversibility __
P. Egocentrism __
Q. Classification __
R. Schema __
S. Script __

Definitions

1. Piaget's second stage of cognitive development, marked by the appearance of language and symbolic function

2. The ability to concentrate on one stimulus and ignore extraneous stimuli

3. Reasoning that proceeds from specific cases to the formation of a general rule

4. Reasoning that begins with a general rule and then is applied to specific cases

5. Preoperational reasoning in which young children reason from particular to particular

6. The process of placing objects in size order

7. The process of placing objects in different classes

8. The concept that quantities remain the same despite changes in their appearance

9. The tendency to attend to only one dimension at a time

10. Beginning at the end of an operation and working one's way back to the start

11. Children's self-centered belief that everyone is experiencing the world the way that they do

12. The preschooler's belief that everything, animate or inanimate, is conscious or alive

13. The belief that natural phenomena are caused by humans

14. People's knowledge of their own memory processes

15. The use of educational strategies in an attempt to reduce or eliminate some perceived difference between groups

16. A federally funded compensatory education program aimed at reducing or eliminating differences in achievement between disadvantaged and middle-class children

17. Statements of comparison

18. An organized body of knowledge that functions as a framework for describing objects and relationships

19. A structure that describes an appropriate sequence of events in a particular context

Answers

A. 9	B. 12	C. 14
D. 1	E. 6	F. 17
G. 3	H. 8	I. 2
J. 4	K. 16	L. 13
M. 5	N. 15	O. 10
P. 11	Q. 7	R. 18
S. 19		

Self-test: Multiple Choice

1. The preschool child grows about __ inches a year.
a. 3
b. 5
c. 7
d. 9

2. After scribbling, children are most likely to draw
a. animals.
b. shapes.
c. people.
d. houses.

3. The preferred adult response to a preschooler's request for an evaluation of his or her drawing is
a. an objective critique.
b. asking what it is a picture of.
c. asking him or her to tell you about the picture.
d. correcting any errors made in the drawing.

4. Regarding their food intake, most children do not show a preference for
a. sugar.
b. fat.
c. salt.
d. vegetables.

5. Piaget called the stage of cognitive development between two and seven years
a. formal operational.
b. preoperational.
c. operational.
d. preconventional.

6. The key to this second stage of cognitive development is
a. conservation.
b. symbolic function.
c. bilingualism.
d. deductive reasoning.

7. Ordering sticks according to their size is called
a. classification.
b. seriation.
c. centering.
d. transformation.

8. Egocentrism, as defined by Piaget, indicates
a. selfishness.
b. self-confidence.
c. impulsivity.
d. self-centeredness.

9. Thinking that the toilet is angry exemplifies
a. egocentrism.
b. artificialism.
c. animism.
d. irreversibility.

10. Children are more likely to pay attention to something if
a. it makes noise.
b. it is novel.
c. they can understand it.
d. all of the above

11. Scripts and schemata show how _____ affects the way children process new information.
a. prior knowledge
b. imitation
c. reinforcement
d. a parent

12. Preschoolers view about ___ hours a day of television.
a. 2
b. 3
c. 4
d. 5

Self-test: True False

_1. A child's rate of growth is fairly regular over time.

_2. Boys generally have more muscle tissue than girls, and girls typically have more fat tissue.

_3. About a quarter of all males and females are left handed.

_4. Accidents are the leading cause of death in the preschool years.

_5. The most important meal for preschoolers is lunch.

_6. Concentrating on only one dimension at a time is called centering.

_7. Under certain circumstances, preschoolers can solve problems that Piaget did not think they could.

_8. Children generally ignore the contents of TV commercials.

_9. Children in lower-income groups benefit the most from nursery school.

_10. Head Start programs have not fulfilled their promise.

_11. Parental use of language is the key to children's cognitive advancement.

_12. Sesame Street has been criticized for its fast pacing and depiction of negative behaviors.

_13. Mr. Roger's Neighborhood has been criticized for its slow pacing and lack of appeal to some children.

_14. About half of all four-year-olds attend nursery school.

_15. The most controversial changes in kindergarten have involved full versus half day sessions.

Answers

Multiple Choice

1. A	7. B
2. B	8. D
3. C	9. C
4. D	10. D
5. B	11. A
6. B	12. B

True False

1. T	8. F
2. T	9. T
3. F	10. F
4. T	11. T
5. F	12. T
6. T	13. T
7. T	14. T
	15. F

Challenge Questions

1. How might a parent's criticisms inadvertently inhibit a child's self-expression?

_____
_____
_____
_____
_____
_____
_____
_____

2. One of the perpetual struggles between parents and children involves the child's diet. How firm should parents be in regulating their children's food intake? Why is it particularly important that children learn good eating habits at an early age?

_____
_____
_____
_____
_____
_____
_____
_____

_____
_____
_____

3. Imagine not being able to understand the causes of common life events like birth and death. What aspects of preoperational thought limit a child's understanding of reality?

_____
_____
_____
_____
_____
_____
_____
_____

4. What limits, if any, would you place on your child's television watching? What would you tell your child about commercials? What effects might the graphic portrayal of sex and violence on cable TV have on young children?

_____
_____
_____
_____
_____
_____
_____
_____
_____

Chapter Activities

1. Watch a few children's television programs. What might children learn from the content of these programs? How much violence is portrayed? What kinds of commercials are shown? How do they appeal to children's needs and desires? What recommendations can you make regarding improving the programming for children?

2. Based on your reading of the **InfoTrac** articles listed below (and textbook chapter 8), describe how developmental psychologists study cognitive development in children, especially memory, attention, and thinking. Do the specific wording of the questions researchers ask children influence what children reveal about what they know? How aware are children of their own cognitions? In your opinion, do parents typically underestimate or overestimate what their children know?

Bruck, M. & Ceci, S.J. (1999). The suggestibility of children's memory. *Annual Review of Psychology*, p. 419.

Flavell, J.H. (1999). Cognitive development: Children's knowledge about the mind. *Annual Review of Psychology*, p. 21.

Memon, A. & Vartoukian, R. (1996). The effects of repeated questioning on young children's eyewitness testimony. *British Journal of Psychology, 87,* p. 403 (13).

Kennedy, J.M. (1996). Children drawing people. *American Journal of Psychology, 109,* p. 150 (8).

3. Based on the **InfoTrac** articles cited below, discuss the following: What do we know about children's nutritional needs? Are these needs currently being met? What are some possible long-term consequences of poor nutrition during childhood? Is it safe for female adolescents to diet to maintain a slim figure? What can parents do to improve their children's diets?

Harnack, L., Stang, J., & Story, M. (1999). Soft drink consumption among U.S. children and adolescents: Nutritional consequences. *Journal of the American Dietetic Association, 99,* p. 436 (6).

Neumark-Sztainer, D., Story, M., Resnick, M.D., & Blum, R.W. (1998). Lessons learned about adolescent nutrition from the Minnesota Adolescent Health Survey. *Journal of the American Dietetic Association, 98,* p. 1449 (8).

Pesa, J. (1999). Psychosocial factors associated with dieting behaviors among female adolescents. *Journal of School Health, 69,* p. 196.

Shaw, M.E. (1998). Adolescent breakfast skipping: An Australian study. *Adolescence, 33,* p. 851 (1).

Williams, C.L., Bollella, M., Boccia, L., & Spark, A. (1998). Dietary fat and children's health. *Nutrition Today, 33,* p. 144 (12).

Position of the American Dietetic Association: Dietary guidance for healthy children aged 2 to 11 years. (1999). *Journal of the American Dietetic Assocation, 99,* p. 93 (9).

CHAPTER NINE

Social *and* Personality Development *in* Early Childhood

Chapter Objectives

After studying Chapter Nine of the text, you should be able to:

* describe Erikson's third stage of psychosocial development, initiative versus guilt.

* describe the emergence of the self-concept during infancy and early childhood.

* discuss the emotional life of preschoolers, and list common childhood fears.

* define play and describe the developmental benefits of various types of early childhood play.

* describe what play behavior reveals about children's cognitive development.

* interpret the research on sex differences in play.

* describe several different parenting styles and their relation to how children "turn out."

* distinguish between the power-assertive and love-oriented discipline styles.

* distinguish between discipline and punishment.

* describe how parenting styles vary according to culture and subculture.

* describe how sibling relationships may affect children, and what parents can do to discourage unnecessary sibling conflict.

* discuss the role of heredity and rearing in understanding why siblings typically are so different from each other.

* discuss the advantages and disadvantages of being an only child.

* describe the preschooler's peer relationships and the beginnings of friendships.

* predict the levels of preschool prosocial behavior and conflict in preschoolers' relationships.

* describe the nature of conflict in young children.

* list consistent gender differences observed in preschool children.

* distinguish between gender identity, gender stability, and gender consistency.

* discuss the biological and learning factors that appear to influence gender development.

* distinguish between different forms of child abuse, and the causes and effects of each type.

* discuss the hazards of using harsh punishment with children.

* review what can be done to prevent child abuse.

Study Questions

Consider these questions **before** you read the chapter:

1. What are the most common fears of childhood? How should parents respond to these fears?

2. What types of experiences contribute to children's concept of self?

3. Describe the potential benefits of play, including dramatic play, in the following domains of development.
    a. physical development
    b. interpersonal skills
    c. problem-solving
    d. emotional development

4. How does play change as children develop cognitively?

5. What gender differences exist in children's play?

6. When siblings fight, should parents intervene? Explain.

7. What is the nature of preschool friendships?

8. How do children acquire gender role identities?

9. Distinguish between discipline and punishment.

10. Should punishment be used as a discipline strategy? If so, how can it be used effectively?

11. What is the profile of an abusive parent?

12. What can parents do to protect their children from being sexually abused?

Study Questions Review

After you have studied Chapter Nine, fill in this section.

1. What are the most common fears of childhood? How should parents respond to these fears?

_____
_____
_____
_____
_____
_____
_____
_____
_____
_____
_____

2. What types of experiences contribute to children's concept of self?

_____
_____
_____
_____
_____
_____
_____
_____

3. Describe the potential benefits of play, including dramatic play, in the following domains of development.
a. physical development
b. interpersonal skills
c. problem-solving
d. emotional development

_____
_____
_____
_____
_____
_____
_____
_____
_____
_____
_____
_____
_____
_____

4. How does play change as children develop cognitively?

_____
_____
_____
_____
_____
_____
_____
_____
_____

5. What gender differences exist in children's play?

_____
_____
_____
_____
_____
_____
_____
_____
_____
_____
_____

6. When siblings fight, should parents intervene? Explain.

_____
_____
_____
_____
_____
_____
_____
_____

7. What is the nature of preschool friendships?

_____
_____
_____
_____
_____
_____
_____

8. How do children acquire gender role identities?

_____
_____
_____
_____
_____
_____
_____
_____
_____

9. Distinguish between discipline and punishment.

_____
_____
_____
_____
_____
_____
_____
_____

10. Should punishment be used as a discipline strategy? If so, how can it be used effectively?

_____
_____
_____
_____
_____
_____
_____
_____
_____
_____

11. What is the profile of an abusive parent?

_____
_____
_____
_____
_____
_____
_____
_____
_____
_____

12. What can parents do to protect their children from being sexually abused?

_____
_____
_____
_____
_____
_____
_____
_____
_____

Important Terms and Concepts

Match the term to its definition below

A. Child neglect __   R. Discipline __
B. Post traumatic stress disorder __   S. Love-oriented discipline __
C. Punishment __   T. Sex typing __
D. Altruism __   U. Onlooker play __
E. Self-concept __   V. Authoritative parenting __
F. Identification __   W. Parallel play __
G. Initiative versus guilt __   X. Social cognition __
H. Authoritarian parenting __   Y. Associative play __
I. Child abuse __   Z. Pretend (dramatic) play __
J. Gender differences __
K. Unoccupied behavior __
L. Prosocial behavior __
M. Power assertive discipline __
N. Displacement __
O. Emotional (psychological) abuse __
P. Solitary play __
Q. Permissive parenting style __

Definitions

1. Erikson's third stage of psychosocial development, during which the child is an active experimenter

2. A psychological disorder marked by symptoms including flashbacks, sleep difficulties, and a diminished ability to concentrate

3. A type of play in which children stand around, look at others, or perform movements that are not goal directed

4. Independent play in which the child shows no interest in the activities of others

5. A classification of play in which the child watches others play and shows some interest, but is unable to join in

6. A type of play common in two-year-olds in which they play in the presence of other children but not with them

7. A type of play seen in preschoolers who are actively involved with one another but cannot sustain these interactions

8. Play in which children take on the roles of others

9. The relationship between cognition and both knowledge about and behavior regarding social interactions

10. Voluntary actions that are intended to help or benefit another individual or group

11. A type of prosocial behavior that involves actions that help people and for which no reward is expected

12. A style of parenting in which parents rigidly control their children's behavior and value obedience above all else

13. A style of parenting marked by open communication and a lack of parental demand for good behavior

14. A style of parenting in which parents establish limits but allow open communication and some freedom for children to sometimes make their own decisions

15. An attempt to control others in order to hold undesirable impulses in check and to encourage self-control

16. The process by which some physical or emotional pain is inflicted in order to reduce the probability that misbehavior will recur

17. A type of discipline relying on the use of power

18. A type of discipline relying on the use of reasoning and love

19. A general term used to denote injury that is intentionally perpetrated on a child

20. A term used to describe a situation in which the care and supervision of a child is insufficient or improper

21. Psychological damage perpetrated on a child by parental actions which often involve rejection, isolation, terrorizing, ignoring, or corrupting

22. The process by which an emotion is transferred from one object or person to another, more acceptable substitute

23. The process by which people acquire, value, and behave in a manner appropriate to one sex more than the other

24. The differences between males and females that have been established through scientific investigation.

25. Process by which children take on the characteristics of another person, most often a parent

26. The picture people have of themselves

Answers

A. 20	B. 2	C. 16
D. 11	E. 26	F. 25
G. 1	H. 12	I. 19
J. 24	K. 3	L. 10
M. 17	N. 22	O. 21
P. 4	Q. 13	R. 15
S. 18	T. 23	U. 5
W. 6	X. 9	Y. 7
Z. 8		

Self-test: Multiple Choice

1. The stage of social development that Erikson associates with preschool children is called
a. trust versus mistrust.
b. initiative versus guilt.
c. identity versus confusion.
d. none of the above

2. In addition to having fun, children at play also benefit in the following way
a. encouraging physical and motor abilities.
b. learning social skills.
c. self-expression and coping skills.
d. all of the above.

3. Authoritative parents
a. encourage obedience above all else.
b. make few demands.
c. use reasoning and persuasion.
d. are harsh and critical.

4. Authoritarian parents
a. threaten to use force.
b. are warm and accepting.
c. value independence in their children.
d. all of the above

5. Permissive parents
a. tend to be emotionally abusive.
b. do not attempt to regulate their children's behavior.
c. establish tough rules and regulations.
d. are power oriented.

6. Punishment, by definition,
a. weakens behavior.
b. strengthens desirable behavior.
c. teaches self-control.
d. encourages obedience.

7. Most children can understand the labels boy and girl by the age of
a. 2.
b. 3.
c. 4.
d. 5.

8. The most clear-cut gender difference is
a. aggression.
b. verbal ability.
c. attention span.
d. coordination.

9. The fact that males are generally more aggressive and competitive than females can be attributable
to
a. genes
b. hormones
c. rearing
d. all of the above

10. Self concept is
a. absent at birth.
b. cumulative.
c. partly based on feedback from others.
d. all of the above

11. Playing in the presence of others, but not with them is called
a. onlooker play.
b. unoccupied play.
c. solitary play.
d. parallel play.

12. The type of play most parents and teachers discourage is
a. dramatic play.
b. rough and tumble play.
c. associative play.
d. role playing.

13. Preschool friendships tend to be
a. fragile.
b. permanent.
c. intimate.
d. competitive.

14. About what percent of children have siblings?
a. 20
b. 40
c. 60
d. 80

Self-test: True-False

_1. Children engage in play activities for pleasure.

_2. Parallel play precedes onlooker play.

_3. Boys generally play more roughly than girls.

_4. Girls rarely act aggressively toward one another.

_5. Cooperation and competition increase with age.

_6. Removing a positive reinforcer is considered punishment.

_7. Abusive parents tend to be either drug addicts or mentally ill.

_8. Teasing children about their fears in the presence of their friends helps them cope.

_9. Infants are able to recognize themselves in the mirror.

_10. Pretend play may begin as early as the second year.

_11. Rough and tumble play is the same as aggressive play.

_12. Sex differences in play are well-documented.

_13. It is very rare for seven- and eight-year-olds to have friends of the opposite sex.

_14. Most sibling conflicts are settled without adult intervention.

_15. Competition and rivalry between siblings is normal.

_16. Children of authoritative parents tend to be the most self-reliant.

_17. There is little that parents can do to prevent their children from being sexually abused.

_18. Parents can severely damage their children even without hitting them.

Answers

Multiple Choice

1. B	8. A
2. D	9. D
3. C	10. D
4. A	11. D
5. B	12. B
6. A	13. A
7. A	14. D

True False

1. T	10. T
2. F	11. F
3. T	12. T
4. F	13. T
5. T	14. T
6. T	15. T
7. F	16. T
8. F	17. F
9. F	18. T

Challenge Questions

1. "Play is the work of the child." Interpret this statement as it applies to the value of play in development.

_____

_____

_____

_____

_____

_____

_____

2. How is child play different from adult play? How are they alike?

_____

_____

_____

_____

_____

_____

_____

3. Is conflict between siblings ever beneficial? What can children learn from such conflict?

_____

_____

_____

_____

_____

_____

_____

4. Is the use of punishment justifiable in child rearing? What unintentional side-effects might occur if punishment is overly used?

_____

_____

_____

_____

_____

_____

_____

Chapter Activities

1. Visit a laundromat, supermarket, or shopping mall and observe parents interacting with their young children (younger than 5 years). Can you identify parents using any of the parenting styles of discipline described in this chapter? Which parents seem to be more in control? What do you think children are learning from discipline encounters with their parents?

2. Based on your reading of your text and the **InfoTrac** articles listed below, discuss the following: Is there a difference between corporal punishment (e.g., spanking a child) and child abuse? Should parents ever hit a child? How would you, as a parent, discipline your child for a serious offense?
Benatar, D. (1998, Summer). Corporal punishment. *Social Theory and Practice*, p. 237 (1).
Larzelere, R.E. (1996). A review of the outcomes of parental use of nonabusive or customary physical punishment. *Pediatrics, 98,* p. 824 (5).
Lowenthal, B. (1999). Effects of maltreatment and ways to promote children's resiliency. *Childhood Education, 75,* p. 204 (6).

3. How do children learn to identify with and practice a gender role (male or female)? Based on your reading of your text and the two **InfoTrac** articles cited below, evaluate the influence of family, peers, and cultural variables on the acquisition of gender role attitudes in children. Should parents socialize their children according to gender, or should parents practice a gender free (androgynous) rearing style? What would you do? Defend your opinion.
Ex, C.T.G.M. & Janssens, M.A.M. (1998). Maternal influence on daughters' gender role attitudes. *Sex Roles: A Journal of Research, 38,* p. 171 (16).
Witt, S.D. (1997). Parental influence on children's socialization to gender roles. *Adolescence, 32,* p. 253 (7).

CHAPTER TEN

Physical *and* Cognitive Development *in* Middle Childhood

Chapter Objectives

After studying Chapter Ten of the text, you should be able to:

* describe the nature of growth patterns during middle childhood.

* discuss the nutritional needs of children during middle childhood.

* explain the causes of growth problems and obesity.

* evaluate the physical fitness status of children in middle childhood.

* describe the importance of health education in elementary school.

* evaluate the pros and cons of competition in organized sports.

* describe the patterns of motor skill development in middle childhood.

* distinguish between the cognitive abilities of preschool children in the preoperational stage and those of elementary school age children in concrete operations.

* summarize the limitations of concrete operational thought.

* analyze the research on memory improvement during middle childhood.

* discuss the changes in information processing abilities in school age children.

* define metamemory and give examples of how its study can help us understand children's memory and task performance.

* describe the advances in linguistic ability during the elementary school years.

* discuss the relationships between reasoning and humor.

* describe the modern approaches to the teaching of reading, writing, and math skills.

* relate computer literacy to children's educational curriculum.

* summarize current views about the effectiveness of the nation's elementary schools.

* describe how creativity can be encouraged at home and in the classroom.

* analyze the key factors that affect school performance.

* discuss various models of intelligence and describe how intelligence tests might be misused.

* compare achievement patterns in male and female elementary school children.

* discuss the special abilities, needs, and problems of bilingual children.

* discuss the issues surrounding the teaching of ebonics.

* discuss different types of disabilities found in children and efforts to help children with special needs.

Study Questions

Consider these questions **before** you read the chapter:

1. How does physical growth vary according to gender during middle childhood?

2. Should school-aged children decide for themselves what to eat? Why are so many young children overweight today?

3. In what ways are school-age children more advanced in motor development than preschool children?

4. What are the potential advantages for children in participating in organized sports? The potential disadvantages?

5. Why did Piaget label the third stage of cognitive development, concrete operational thought?

6. In what sense are elementary school children less self centered than preschool children?

7. How do children demonstrate conservation of
   a. number?
   b. substance?
   c. weight?
   d. volume?

8. What are the main limitations of concrete operational thinking?

9. How do the changes that occur in recall and recognition memory during the school years affect the way children can be taught?

10. Does the average 5th grader understand what he or she is saying when reciting the pledge of allegiance? Explain.

11. How do children's conversations differ from those of adolescents or adults?

12. What are the benefits for school-aged children of having a sense of humor?

13. How do reading and computer literacy encourage children's cognitive growth?

14. What are the main criticisms of elementary schools today?

15. How does poverty usually affect children's school performance?

16. Describe how intelligence tests are designed, used, and sometimes misused.

17. Why do many bilingual children struggle to achieve in school?

18. What is the main purpose of mainstreaming children with special needs?

19. What are the most common forms of learning disability?

20. What does it mean to be gifted and talented?

Study Questions Review

After you have studied Chapter Ten, fill in this section.

1. How does physical growth vary according to gender during middle childhood?

_____
_____
_____
_____
_____
_____
_____
_____
_____

2. Should school-aged children decide for themselves what to eat? Why are so many young children overweight today?

_____
_____
_____
_____
_____
_____
_____
_____
_____
_____

3. In what ways are school-age children more advanced in motor development than preschool children?

_____
_____
_____
_____
_____
_____
_____
_____
_____
_____

4. What are the potential advantages for children in participating in organized sports? The potential disadvantages?

_____

_____

_____

_____

_____

_____

_____

_____

_____

5. Why did Piaget label the third stage of cognitive development, concrete operational thought?

_____

_____

_____

_____

6. In what sense are elementary school children less self centered than preschool children?

_____

_____

_____

_____

_____

_____

_____

7. How do children demonstrate conservation of
   a. number?
   b. substance?
   c. weight?
   d. volume?

_____

_____

_____

_____

_____

_____

_____

_____
_____
_____
_____
_____
_____

8. What are the main limitations of concrete operational thinking?

_____
_____
_____
_____
_____
_____
_____
_____
_____
_____

9. How do the changes that occur in recall and recognition memory during the school years affect the way children can be taught?

_____
_____
_____
_____
_____
_____
_____
_____
_____
_____

10. Does the average 5th grader understand what he or she is saying when reciting the pledge of allegiance? Explain.

_____
_____
_____
_____
_____

11. How do children's conversations differ from those of adolescents or adults?

_____

_____

_____

_____

_____

_____

_____

12. What are the benefits for school-aged children of having a sense of humor?

_____

_____

_____

_____

_____

_____

_____

_____

_____

13. How do reading and computer literacy encourage children's cognitive growth?

_____

_____

_____

_____

_____

_____

_____

_____

14. What are the main criticisms of elementary schools today?

_____

_____

_____

_____

_____

_____

_____

15. How does poverty usually affect children's school performance?

_____
_____
_____
_____
_____
_____
_____
_____
_____

16. Describe how intelligence tests are designed, used, and sometimes misused.

_____
_____
_____
_____
_____
_____
_____
_____
_____

17. Why do many bilingual children struggle to achieve in school?

_____
_____
_____
_____
_____
_____
_____
_____
_____

18. What is the main purpose of mainstreaming children with special needs?

_____
_____
_____
_____
_____
_____
_____

19. What are the most common forms of learning disability?

_____
_____
_____
_____
_____
_____
_____
_____
_____

20. What does it mean to be gifted and talented?

_____
_____
_____
_____
_____
_____
_____
_____
_____

Important Terms and Concepts

Match the term to its definition below

A. Mental age __
B. Intelligence __
C. Mental retardation __
D. Metamemory __
E. Learning disability __
F. Concrete operational stage __
G. Computer literacy __
H. Attention-deficit/hyperactivity disorder (ADHD) __
I. Mainstreaming __
J. Deciduous teeth __
K. Intelligence quotient (IQ) __
L. Horizontal decalage __
M. Ebonics __
N. Metacognition __
O. Theory of multiple intelligences __
P. Full inclusion __

Definitions

1. The ability to benefit from experience, solve problems, or do well in school

2. A condition marked by subnormal intellectual functioning and adjustment difficulties

3. The scientific term for 'baby teeth'

4. Piaget's third stage of cognitive development, in which children can think logically about concrete objects and events

5. A term used to describe the unevenness of development in which children may be able to solve one type of problem but not another, even though a common principle underlies them all

6. A person's knowledge of his or her own memory process

7. The conscious monitoring and regulation of the way people approach and solve a problem

8. A term used to describe general knowledge about computers

9. A type of linguistic communication used by some African-Americans

10. Howard Gardner's view that there are seven types of intelligence

11. A condition used to describe children who are impulsive, easily distracted, and overly active

12. The age at which an individual is functioning intellectually

13. A score that permits an individual's performance on an intelligence test to be compared to the typical performance of same-aged individuals

14. The practice of placing disabled students into regular classrooms

15. A group of disorders marked by significant difficulties in listening, speaking, reading, writing, reasoning and math

16. The movement to provide special services for all children with disabilities in regular classrooms

Answers

Self-test: Multiple Choice

1. Girls are heavier than boys at around age
a. 5.
b. 7.
c. 9.
d. 14.

2. Children's food preferences are mainly influenced by
a. friends.
b. television advertising.
c. parental modeling.
d. health education in school.

3. Obese children usually
a. have few friends.
b. have a poor body image.
c. become obese adults.
d. all of the above

4. The least helpful intervention for obese children is
a. heavy dieting.
b. increased exercise.
c. teaching social skills.
d. parental support.

5. Any sex differences in athletic ability observed in middle childhood are likely to be due to
a. size differences.
b. training and motivation.
c. larger muscles in boys.
d. hormonal differences.

6. Children in the concrete operational stage become less
a. active.
b. curious.
c. logical.
d. egocentric.

7. Children in the concrete operational stage still show deficits in
a. vocabulary.
b. thinking about numbers.
c. thinking about hypothetical situations.
d. attention.

8. Taking into account more than one dimension of a problem is called
a. reversibility
b. decentering
c. seriation
d. metamemory

9. Poor reading habits usually can be attributed to
a. excessive television watching.
b. the child's attitudes about reading.
c. values taught at home.
d. all of the above

10. Today, I.Q. tests are used primarily for
a. placement.
b. remediation.
c. diagnosis.
d. parental awareness.

11. What aspect of computers has become the focus of computer education?
a. computer history
b. terminology
c. programming
d. applications

12. Culture fair intelligence tests depend more heavily on
a. language abilities.
b. speed of responding.
c. matching, copying, and picture completion.
d. cultural experiences.

13. The Education for All Handicapped Children Act
a. applies to gifted children.
b. requires mainstreaming of disabled children.
c. mandates that children be placed in the least restrictive environment.
d. minimizes the role of parents in their children's educational plans.

14. Hyperactive children are typically
a. impulsive.
b. easily distracted.
c. poorly behaved.
d. all of the above

Self-Test: True-False

_1. Poor eating habits have little to do with school performance.

_2. Obese children usually become normally weighted adults.

_3. Most school-aged children would rather be physically active than watch TV or play video games.

_4. Boys benefit more than girls from being physically fit.

_5. Children of different cultures may achieve concrete operational thought at different ages.

_6. Young children often believe that they know and understand more than they actually do.

_7. Poor reading skills often reflect excessive television watching.

_8. Children's writing is most beneficial when it is based on their own experiences.

_9. Errors of punctuation and spelling should be a teacher's main priority when teaching children how to write.

_10. Most organized sports minimize competition.

_11. Girls excel in tasks that require agility, rhythm, and hopping.

_12. The shift from preoperational to concrete operation thinking is sudden.

_13. School-aged children have little difficulty reasoning about hypothetical situations.

_14. The most fundamental academic skill is math

_15. Children who can count are showing that they understand the idea of quantity.

_16. American students generally know very little about computers.

_17. Girls generally excel in verbal activities and boys generally excel in math.

_18. Modern theorists agree that what we call intelligence is actually several different abilities.

Answers

Multiple Choice

1. C	8. B
2. B	9. D
3. D	10. C
4. A	11. D
5. B	12. C
6. D	13. C
7. C	14. D

True-False

1. F	10. F
2. F	11. T
3. F	12. F
4. F	13. F
5. T	14. F
6. T	15. F
7. F	16. T
8. T	17. T
9. F	18. T

Challenge Questions

1. What can parents do to encourage their children's physical fitness?

_____

_____

_____

_____

_____

_____

_____

_____

2. How is the thinking of school-aged children similar to that of adults? How is it different? How might the differences affect adult-child communication?

_____

_____

_____

_____

_____

_____

_____

_____

_____

_____

3. If you were an English teacher, how would you encourage creative writing in your students?

_____

_____

_____

_____

_____

_____

_____

4. Computers are becoming more common in classrooms. What aspects of computers make them so appealing to youngsters? Why do boys appear to be more interested in computers than girls?

_____

_____

_____

_____

_____

_____

_____

_____

_____

5. Is society doing enough to help children with learning problems? What steps would you take to improve their educational opportunities if you were in charge?

_____

_____

_____
_____
_____
_____
_____
_____
_____
_____
_____
_____

Chapter Activities

1. Replicate Piaget's conservation studies with children of different ages. For example, arrange two equal rows of M&M candies with one row more spread out than the other. Ask the children which row has more candy. Make sure you understand and have practiced the procedures and that you know what questions you will ask. Report your findings.

2. Using the **InfoTrac** search function, locate one article addressing each of the following topics, and summarize the main conclusions of each article: bilingual education, giftedness, childhood obesity, computer literacy, and creativity in children.

Social *and* Personality Development *in* Middle Childhood

Chapter Objectives

After studying Chapter Eleven of the text, you should be able to:

* describe how Erikson and Freud viewed the middle childhood years.

* define the terms "self-concept" and "self-esteem" and outline the process by which self-concept develops.

* discuss ways of enhancing a school-aged child's self-esteem.

* summarize the changes in child-rearing strategies and in the parent-child relationship during middle childhood.

* describe the advantages to children when their parents are able to work as partners in parenting.

* summarize the typical short- and long-term effects on children of parental divorce.

* describe how the effects of divorce on children vary according to a child's age and gender.

* describe the potential strengths and weaknesses of single parent families.

* discuss the myths and realities of stepfamily life.

* describe the special problems of children in self-care.

* describe how homeless families are similar to, and different from, other poor families.

* describe why some children are more resilient to stress than others.

* summarize our current understanding of families led by gay and lesbian parents.

* list the factors that are associated with children's popularity and unpopularity.

* discuss the nature of the changes in children's friendships during middle childhood.

* compare and evaluate Kohlberg's and Piaget's models of moral reasoning.

* compare and evaluate the psychoanalytic and learning models of moral behavior.

* describe what parents and teachers can do to encourage moral and prosocial behavior.

* list the key factors that appear to encourage aggressive behavior in children.

* interpret the research on the influence of television violence on children's aggressiveness.

* describe the profile of resilient (stress-resistant) children.

Study Questions

Consider these questions **before** you read the chapter:

1. To Erikson, what is the key developmental challenge of middle childhood?

2. How does self-concept change over the course of childhood?

3. How might a child's self-esteem be related to his or her performance in school?

4. During middle childhood, what changes occur in children's relationships with their family members?

5. What changes in family life during middle childhood encourage children to become more independent?

6. Describe the typical immediate, short- and long-term effects of divorce on children. What difference do the age and sex of the child make?

7. How are stepfamilies different from single-parent and nuclear families?

8. What distinctive problems do homeless children have?

9. What can children learn about relationships and about themselves from interacting with their peers?

10. What characteristics of children influence their popularity with peers? What can parents do if their children are unpopular with their age-mates?

11. In what ways does friendship change with age?

12. How do gender roles evolve during middle childhood?

13. How do children develop a sense of what is right and wrong? What role do their parents play?

14. What factors appear to promote aggressive behavior?

15. What are the common stressors of middle childhood? How do children cope with these stressors?

Study Questions Review

After you have studied Chapter Eleven, fill in this section.

1. To Erikson, what is the key developmental challenge of middle childhood?

_____
_____
_____
_____
_____

2. How does self-concept change over the course of childhood?

_____
_____
_____
_____
_____
_____
_____
_____
_____

3. How might a child's self-esteem be related to his or her performance in school?

_____
_____
_____
_____

_____
_____
_____
_____
_____
_____

4. During middle childhood, what changes typically occur in children's relationships with their family members?

_____
_____
_____
_____
_____
_____
_____
_____
_____
_____

5. What changes in family life during middle childhood encourage children to become more independent?

_____
_____
_____
_____
_____
_____
_____
_____
_____
_____

6. Describe the typical immediate, short- and long-term effects of divorce on children. What difference do the age and sex of the child make?

_____
_____
_____
_____
_____
_____
_____
_____

7. How are stepfamilies different from single-parent and nuclear families?

_____
_____
_____
_____
_____
_____
_____
_____
_____
_____

8. What distinctive problems do homeless children have?

_____
_____
_____
_____
_____
_____
_____
_____
_____
_____

9. What can children learn about relationships and about themselves from interacting with their peers?

_____
_____
_____
_____
_____
_____
_____
_____
_____

10. What characteristics of children influence their popularity with peers? What can parents do if their children are unpopular with their age-mates?

_____
_____
_____
_____

11. In what ways does friendship change with age?

12. How do gender roles evolve during middle childhood?

13. How do children develop a sense of what is right and wrong? What role do their parents play?

14. What factors appear to promote aggressive behavior?

_____
_____
_____
_____
_____
_____
_____

15. What are the common stressors of middle childhood? How do children cope with these stressors?

_____
_____
_____
_____
_____
_____
_____
_____
_____
_____

Important Terms and Concepts

Match the term to its definition below:

A. Superego __
B. Self-esteem __
C. Moral realism __
D. Moral reasoning __
E. Self-care (latchkey) children __
F. Preconventional level __
G. Industry versus inferiority __
H. Latency stage __
I. Conventional level __
J. Resilient children __
K. Moral relativism __
L. Postconventional level __
M. Self-concept __
N. Ego ideal __

Definitions

1. Erikson's fourth psychosocial stage, emphasizing competency and achievement

2. Freud's fourth psychosexual stage, during which sexuality is hidden or dormant

3. The judgments and values people place on various aspects of their self

4. Elementary schoolchildren who must care for themselves before or after school hours

5. Children who do not appear to be negatively affected by stress, or are at least able to cope well despite extreme stress

6. An approach to the study of moral development stressing the importance of the child's ideas and reasoning about justice and right and wrong

7. The Piagetian stage of moral reasoning during which rules are viewed as sacred and justice is whatever the authority figure says

8. The Piagetian stage of moral reasoning in which children weigh the intentions of others before judging their actions to be right or wrong

9. Kohlberg's first stage of moral reasoning, based on satisfaction of one's own needs and reward and punishment

10. Kohlberg's second stage of moral reasoning, in which individuals conform to the expectations of others

11. Kohlberg's third stage of moral reasoning, in which moral decisions are based on individual conscience

12. The portion of the mind in psychoanalytic theory corresponding to the standards of conduct we have learned from our caregivers

13. The picture people have of themselves, who they think they are

14. The individual's positive and desirable standards of behavior

Answers

A. 12	B. 3	C. 7
D. 6	E. 4	F 9
G. 1	H. 2	I. 10
J. 5	K. 8	L. 11
M. 13	N. 14	

Self-test: Multiple Choice

1. The positive outcome of Erikson's fourth stage of psychosocial development is
a. trust.
b. industry.
c. mistrust.
d. initiative.

2. According to Freud, children in the latency stage of psychosexual development
a. repress their feelings toward the opposite sex.
b. have a heightened sex drive.
c. identify with the parent of the opposite gender.
d. have major adjustment problems.

3. Children's self-concept during middle childhood reflects
a. feedback they receive from others.
b. a heightened ability to evaluate themselves logically.
c. greater awareness of how others see them.
d. all of the above

4. The most powerful influence on children's development and mental health is
a. their friends.
b. their family.
c. television.
d. their teachers.

5. Self-esteem is our evaluation of our
a. body.
b. personality.
c. self-concept.
d. abilities.

6. Perhaps the key theme running through development during middle childhood is increasing
a. comformity.
b. compliance.
c. popularity.
d. independence.

7. After divorce,
a. children adjust quickly.
b. mothers become more permissive and flexible.
c. behavior problems are likely.
d. children receive a lot of social support.

8. The long-term effects of divorce depend upon
a. the parents' relationship with each other following divorce.
b. the child's age when divorce occurs.
c. whether the child is male or female.
d. all of the above

9. The most complex type of family is the
a. nuclear family.
b. single parent family.
c. foster family.
d. stepfamily.

10. About what percent of children aged five to fourteen years are in self-care?
a. 5
b. 8
c. 12
d. 15

11. Resilient children
a. are particularly vulnerable to stress.
b. are usually flexible and easygoing.
c. are fearful and dependent.
d. focus on the negative aspects of their life situations.

12. Fear of punishment characterizes which stage of Kohlberg's model of moral reasoning?
a. preconventional
b. conventional
c. postconventional
d. all three stages

13. Unpopular children tend to be
a. low achievers.
b. school dropouts.
c. emotionally maladjusted.
d. all of the above

14. During middle childhood, boys and girls
a. do not speak to one another.
b. reject each other.
c. avoid each other.
d. enjoy each other's company.

15. In Freud's model, morality involves the development of the
a. id.
b. ego.
c. superego.
d. brain.

16. Aggressive children
a. are unpopular.
b. have high self-esteem.
c. are about equally male and female.
d. all of the above

17. About how many American children experience stress-related health problems?
a. 10%
b. 25%
c. 35%
d. 45%

Self-test: True-False

__1. After divorce, the custodial parent usually becomes more flexible and permissive.

__2. Most of the initial reactions to divorce diminish or disappear by the end of the first year following the divorce.

__3. Stepfamilies are very similar to nuclear families.

__4. In middle childhood, boys and girls tend to avoid each other.

__5. Girls are more conscious of sex-role behaviors than are boys.

__6. Aggressive children tend to come from violent families.

__7. Self-concept refers to the value a person may place on various aspects of his or her self.

__8. Some homeless children are stress-resistant.

__9. Aggressive children tend to view the world as a hostile place.

__10. Authoritative parents enforce rules and encourage self-reliance.

__11. Parents who agree with each other are usually more effective parents.

__12. Following divorce, mothers and fathers usually become more demanding of their children.

_13. Divorce generally has a greater impact on younger children than older children.

_14. Children typically adjust as well in stepfamilies as in other types of family configurations.

_15. Research suggests that most children in self-care suffer as a result.

_16. Popular children tend to be physically appealing.

Answers
Multiple Choice

1. B	9. D
2. A	10. B
3. D	11. B
4. B	12. A
5. C	13. D
6. D	14. C
7. C	15. C
8. D	16. A
	17. C

True-False

1. F	9. T
2. T	10. T
3. F	11. T
4. T	12. F
5. F	13. F
6. T	14. T
7. F	15. F
8. T	16. T

Challenge Questions

1. There appears to be a strong relationship between parental acceptance of a child, the child's self-esteem, and other important personality qualities. As a parent, how would you communicate with and discipline your child to promote his or her self-liking?

_____

_____

_____

_____

_____

_____

_____

2. Children of divorce suffer a major reduction in parental support just when they need it the most. How can a social support system of siblings, grandparents, friends, neighbors, and teachers compensate for this temporary loss of parental support?

_____
_____
_____
_____
_____
_____
_____
_____
_____
_____
_____
_____
_____

3. With a high rate of divorce and remarriage, stepfamilies are becoming more common. What types of issues would you expect to uncover in stepfamilies regarding
a. discipline?_____
_____
_____
_____
_____
_____
_____

b. divided loyalties?_____
_____
_____
_____
_____
_____

c. sexual boundaries?_____
_____
_____
_____
_____
_____
_____

d. territoriality and living arrangements (if there are stepsiblings)?_____

_____

_____

_____

_____

_____

e. visitation? _____

_____

_____

_____

_____

_____

4. Thinking back to your childhood, what particular traits or qualities of your friends did you value? As an adult, do you still seek the same qualities in your friends?

_____

_____

_____

_____

_____

_____

_____

5. Why is it more acceptable in our culture for a girl to be a "tomboy" than for a boy to be a "sissy?"

_____

_____

_____

_____

_____

_____

_____

6. Based on your reading of this chapter, how would you raise a morally responsible child? Include some discussion about your status as a role model.

_____

_____

_____

_____

_____

_____

_____

_____

_____

_____

_____

_____

_____

_____

Chapter Activities

1. Devise several hypothetical situations involving such immoral behaviors as lying, cheating, stealing, and hitting. Ask children of different ages about the behaviors: are they right or wrong? Ask them to justify (explain) their answers. Try to understand their moral reasoning without judging or influencing their responses.

2. In our very competitive society, children's ability to cope with stress is of particular concern to psychologists. Using your text and at least two **InfoTrac** articles (e.g., Jewett, J. (1997). Childhood stress. *Childhood Education, 73,* p. 172 (2)), discuss common stressors of childhood, children's ability to cope with such stressors, and what parents and teachers can do to help children become more resilient.

3. How well do children and adolescents adjust to their parents' divorce and remarriage? What variables mediate their adjustment? Use the following and other **InfoTrac** articles to address these questions:

Jeynes, W.H. (1999). Effects of remarriage following divorce on the academic achievement of children. *Journal of Youth and Adolescence, 28,* p. 385 (9)

Kim, L.S., Sandler, I.N., & Tein, J-Y. (1997). Locus of control as a stress moderator and mediator in children of divorce. *Journal of Abnormal Child Psychology, 25,* p. 145 (11).

Physical *and* Cognitive Development *in* Adolescence

Chapter Objectives

After studying Chapter Twelve of the text, you should be able to:

* list some popular stereotypes of adolescents and compare them to what adolescents are really like.

* distinguish between puberty and adolescence.

* distinguish between primary and secondary sexual characteristics.

* outline the sequences of physical changes in males and females during adolescence.

* describe girls' typical reactions to the onset of menstruation.

* define the secular trend and theorize about why it is gradually slowing in western societies.

* outline the sequence of events leading to the onset of puberty.

* summarize the research concerning early and late maturation in males and females.

* describe current concerns about the health of adolescents in general.

* profile the adolescent at risk for attempting suicide.

* describe why nutritional needs are greater during adolescence than in any other life stage.

* discuss the relationship between body image and adolescent self-esteem.

* define anorexia nervosa and bulimia and describe the nature of these disorders.

* discuss the special problems facing obese adolescents.

* speculate about why adolescents seem to always be tired.

* describe the cognitive advances of adolescents as characterized by Piaget's concept of formal operations.

* suggest criticisms and limitations of Piaget's formulations.

* describe several facets of adolescent egocentrism and how they distort adolescent thinking.

* summarize the factors that appear to increase the likelihood of adolescent risk taking.

* describe differences between religious and non-religious adolescents.

* summarize the changes in sexual attitudes and behaviors that have occurred over the past decade.

* describe the benefits of dating during adolescence.

* discuss the issues surrounding date and acquaintance rape.

* discuss why adolescents often take sexual risks.

* discuss the controversies surrounding sex education programs, especially regarding the issue of abstinence.

* describe the characteristics of successful sex education programs.

* discuss the problem of teenage pregnancy from the point of view of the baby, the mother, the father and the extended family.

* describe how the threat of AIDS has affected teenage sexuality.

* describe the special problems of gay and lesbian adolescents.

Study Questions

Consider these questions **before** you read the chapter:

1. How are adolescents different from younger children? Different from adults?

2. How do adults view teenagers? Is this view fair or accurate?

3. What is the difference between puberty and adolescence?

4. What physical changes accompany puberty for
   a. males?
   b. females?

5. What should parents tell their daughters about menstruation before its onset?

6. What is the secular trend? How can it be explained?

7. What role do hormones play in triggering the onset of puberty?

8. What social advantages do early maturing boys have over late maturing boys? Are there similar advantages for early maturing girls?

9. What physical characteristics are most valued by adolescent males and females?

10. What are the three most common "poor health habits" of adolescents?

11. Evaluate the success of suicide prevention programs.

12. What psychological factors are associated with the onset of
    a. anorexia nervosa?
    b. bulimia?
    c. obesity?

13. Why do teenagers always seem to be tired?

14. How does the formal operational thinking of the adolescent compare to the reality-bound thinking of younger children?

15. What is the nature of adolescent egocentrism?

16. To what extent is the moral reasoning of the adolescent rooted in cognitive development?

17. Describe some common risk-taking behaviors of adolescence.

18. What role do the following play in influencing moral behavior in adolescents?
    a. situational factors
    b. personality characteristics
    c. family background
    d. cognitive advances

19. What are values? How do adolescents' values compare to those of their parents? What do today's teens value?

20. How do adolescents' religious beliefs affect their behavior?

21. What is the sexual double standard?

22. How well informed are today's adolescents about sexuality?

23. Why do so many teens engage in high risk sexual practices such as avoiding contraceptives?

24. How do most children find out about sex? What do they need to know?

25. What are the potential benefits and risks of dating?

26. Are adolescent mothers and fathers generally competent parents?

27. How do parents typically react upon discovering that their child is gay or lesbian?

Study Questions Review

After you have studied Chapter Twelve, fill in this section.

1. How are adolescents different from younger children? Different from adults?

_____
_____
_____
_____
_____
_____
_____
_____
_____
_____

2. How do adults view teenagers? Is this view fair or accurate?

_____

_____

_____

_____

_____

_____

_____

_____

_____

3. What is the difference between puberty and adolescence?

_____

_____

_____

_____

_____

4. What physical changes accompany puberty for
   a. males?
   b. females?

_____

_____

_____

_____

_____

_____

_____

_____

5. What should parents tell their daughters about menstruation before its onset?

_____

_____

_____

_____

_____

_____

_____

6. What is the secular trend? How can it be explained?

_____

_____

_____

_____

_____

_____

_____

_____

7. What role do hormones play in triggering the onset of puberty?

_____

_____

_____

_____

_____

_____

_____

_____

8. What social advantages do early maturing boys have over late maturing boys? Are there similar advantages for early maturing girls?

_____

_____

_____

_____

_____

_____

_____

_____

9. What physical characteristics are most valued by adolescent males and females?

_____

_____

_____

_____

_____

_____

_____
_____
_____
_____

10. What are the three most common "poor health habits" of adolescents?

_____
_____
_____
_____
_____
_____
_____

11. Evaluate the success of suicide prevention programs.

_____
_____
_____
_____
_____
_____
_____
_____
_____

12. What psychological factors are associated with the onset of
    a. anorexia nervosa?
    b. bulimia?
    c. obesity?

_____
_____
_____
_____
_____
_____
_____
_____

13. Why do teenagers always seem to be tired?

_____
_____
_____
_____
_____
_____
_____

14. How does the formal operational thinking of the adolescent compare to the reality-bound thinking of younger children?

_____
_____
_____
_____
_____
_____
_____

15. What is the nature of adolescent egocentrism?

_____
_____
_____
_____
_____
_____
_____
_____

16. To what extent is the moral reasoning of the adolescent rooted in cognitive development?

_____
_____
_____
_____
_____
_____
_____
_____

_____
_____
_____
_____
_____

17. Describe some common risk-taking behaviors of adolescence.

_____
_____
_____
_____
_____
_____
_____
_____

18. What role do the following play in influencing moral behavior in adolescents?
    a. situational factors
    b. personality characteristics
    c. family background
    d. cognitive advances

_____
_____
_____
_____
_____
_____
_____
_____
_____
_____
_____
_____
_____
_____

19. What are values? How do adolescents' values compare to those of their parents? What do today's teens value?

_____
_____
_____
_____
_____

_____
_____
_____
_____
_____

20. How do adolescents' religious beliefs affect their behavior?

_____
_____
_____
_____
_____
_____
_____
_____

21. What is the sexual double standard?

_____
_____
_____
_____

22. How well informed are today's adolescents about sexuality?

_____
_____
_____
_____
_____
_____
_____
_____

23. Why do so many teens engage in high risk sexual practices such as avoiding contraceptives?

_____
_____
_____
_____
_____
_____

_____
_____
_____

24. How do most children find out about sex? What do they need to know?

_____
_____
_____
_____
_____
_____
_____
_____
_____

25. What are the potential benefits and risks of dating?

_____
_____
_____
_____
_____
_____
_____
_____
_____
_____

26. Are adolescent mothers and fathers generally competent parents?

_____
_____
_____
_____
_____
_____
_____
_____
_____
_____
_____
_____

27. How do parents typically react upon discovering that their child is gay or lesbian?

_____

_____

_____

_____

_____

_____

_____

_____

_____

_____

Important Terms and Concepts

Match the term to its definition below

A. Bulimia __

B. Values __

C. Adolescence __

D. Formal operations __

E. Personal fable __

F. Puberty __

G. Androgens __

H. Primary sexual characteristics __

I. Adolescent egocentrism __

J. Genital stage __

K. Secondary sexual characteristics __

L. Estrogens __

M. Anorexia nervosa __

N. Imaginary audience __

O. Secular trend __

Definitions

1. Physiological changes involved in sexual maturation, as well as other bodily changes that occur during adolescence

2. Body changes directly associated with sexual reproduction

3. Physical changes that distinguish males from females but that are not associated with sexual reproduction

4. The psychological experience of the child from puberty to adulthood

5. The gradual shift toward earlier maturation today, compared with past generations

6. A group of male hormones, including testosterone

7. A group of female hormones, including estradiol

8. A condition of self-imposed starvation found most often among adolescent females

9. An eating disorder marked by episodic binging and purging

10. The fourth Piagetian stage of cognitive development, in which a person develops the ability to deal with abstractions and hypotheses

11.The adolescent failure to differentiate between what one is thinking and what others are considering

12. A term used to describe adolescents' belief that they are the focus of attention and being evaluated by everyone

13. The adolescents' belief that their experiences are unique

14. Constructs that serve as internal guides for behavior

15. The final psychosexual stage, occurring during adolescence, in which adult heterosexual behavior develops

Answers

A. 9	B. 14	C. 4
D. 10	E. 13	F. 1
G. 6	H. 2	I. 11
J. 15	K. 3	L. 7
M. 8	N. 12	O. 5

Self-test: Multiple Choice

1. The key change in puberty involves
a. growth.
b. behavior.
c. fertility.
d. relationships.

2. For males, a primary sex characteristic is
a. body hair.
b. maturation of the testes.
c. deepening of the voice.
d. all of the above

3. For females, the first sign of puberty is usually the
a. growth spurt.
b. first menstruation.
c. development of the breast buds.
d. changes in muscle and fat composition.

4. The first sign of puberty in males is
a. enlargement of the testes and scrotum.
b. the growth spurt.
c. nocturnal emissions.
d. subscribing to the Playboy channel.

5. The secular trend involves generational change in
a. age.
b. height.
c. weight.
d. all of the above

6. Self-imposed starvation is called
a. anorexia.
b. bulimia.
c. bingeing.
d. dyslexia.

7. In Piaget's model, the fourth and final stage of cognitive development is called
a. final operations.
b. formal operations.
c. concrete operations.
d. postconventional.

8. Adolescent thought differs from that of younger children in that it can be more
a. abstract.
b. hypothetical.
c. flexible.
d. all of the above

9. "You don't know what it's like" exemplifies
a. the personal fable.
b. internal locus of control.
c. fear of success.
d. relativistic thinking.

10. The secular trend can be attributed to
a. better health and nutrition.
b. fewer growth-retarding childhood illnesses.
c. better medical care.
d. all of the above

11. Compared to early maturing boys, late maturing boys are considered
a. more masculine.
b. more attractive.
c. better groomed.
d. rebellious and childish.

12. In terms of disease, adolescents can be considered relatively
a. healthy.
b. sickly.
c. malnourished.
d. susceptible.

13. Males who take steroids usually do so to enhance their
a. popularity
b. athletic performance
c. academic performance
d. self image

14. About what percentage of teenagers are obese?
a. 1
b. 2
c. 5
d. 13

15. Anorexics are obsessed with
a. food.
b. weight loss.
c. their appearance.
d. all of the above

16. Which theorist linked moral reasoning to cognitive growth?
a. Freud
b. Erikson
c. Kohlberg
d. Elkind

17. The most common cause of suicide appears to be
a. school failure.
b. loss of boyfriend or girlfriend.
c. depression.
d. drug abuse.

18. About what percentage of adults attain formal operational thought?
a. 20
b. 40
c. 50
d. 80

Self-test: True-False

_1. The growth spurt occurs two years earlier in girls than in boys.

_2. Girls become fertile when they start menstruating.

_3. Females lack the hormone testosterone in their body.

_4. Obese children tend to become obese adults.

_5. Female attitudes toward sex have changed more than male attitudes over the past thirty years.

_6. A majority of today's teens engage in premarital intercourse.

_7. Only about one-third of sexually active teens use contraceptives.

_8. Virtually all college students are capable of formal operational thinking.

_9. Adolescents' values tend to resemble those of their parents.

_10. Freud characterized adolescent sexuality as the phallic stage.

_11. Females generally are more conservative sexually than males.

_12. The most common form of sexual behavior for adolescents is petting.

_13. About 20% of fourteen-year-old girls will become pregnant before reaching the age of eighteen, and over half of them will become pregnant again within three years.

_14. The U.S. has the highest rate of adolescent pregnancy in the West.

_15. The majority of teens learn about sex from their parents or teachers.

_16. Suicide is the leading cause of death among older adolescents.

_17. Not all forms of risk taking are dangerous.

Answers

Multiple Choice

1. C	10. D
2. B	11. D
3. A	12. A
4. A	13. B
5. D	14. D
6. A	15. D
7. B	16. C
8. D	17. C
9. A	18. C

True-False

1. T	9. T
2. F	10. F
3. F	11. T
4. T	12. F
5. T	13. T
6. T	14. T
7. T	15. F
8. F	16. F
	17. T

Challenge Questions

1. Most young adolescents feel awkward and self-conscious about the changes in their bodies accompanying puberty. As a young adolescent, did you feel overly sensitive about some physical characteristic you had, such as your size, pimples, or breasts that you thought were too big or too small? How much time did you spend in front of the mirror, wishing you looked different, and experimenting with styles and mannerisms? How did your feelings about your appearance affect your self-concept?

_____

_____

_____

_____

_____
_____
_____
_____
_____
_____
_____
_____
_____

2. The prevention of eating disorders makes more sense than treating such disorders after they occur. What can parents do to discourage destructive eating patterns in children before they become serious problems?

_____
_____
_____
_____
_____
_____
_____
_____
_____

3. Many of the changes in adolescent behavior that puzzle, frustrate, and sometimes amuse parents can be understood in terms of new cognitive abilities in teens. How might parents who are aware of these changes interpret the following adolescent behaviors?

a. questioning of parents' values _____
_____
_____
_____
_____
_____

b. experimenting with drugs _____
_____
_____
_____
_____
_____

c. body piercing _____
_____

_____

_____

_____

_____

d. imitating hair and dress styles of popular entertainers _____

_____

_____

_____

_____

_____

e. submitting to peer pressure _____

_____

_____

_____

_____

4. There are many issues and controversies surrounding children's and adolescents' sexuality. One of the most provocative involves the staggering statistics involving young, unmarried females who become pregnant. Planned Parenthood maintains that sexually active adolescents should have free access to contraceptives and information about birth control without their parents' knowledge or consent. Others feel this would encourage sexual promiscuity. What do you think?

_____

_____

_____

_____

_____

_____

_____

_____

_____

_____

Chapter Activities

1. By observing popular media, evaluate the pressure on young adolescents to adopt adult attitudes and behaviors. For example, observe the themes and content of music videos and describe what you see. What messages do adolescents get from TV programs, movies, commercials, and other advertising about their sexuality, sex-role expectations, and appropriate behavior? Report your findings.

2. Select five common stereotypes of adolescents and challenge each one using material from this chapter. Do any of these stereotypes have a grain of truth to them? Do any (e.g., materialistic) apply to adults as well as teenagers?

3. How informed are adolescents about human sexuality, including gender differences? What are their attitudes about premarital sexual activity? What do they learn from their parents, peers, and the media? How might misinformation about sex and faulty reasoning affect adolescents' sexual risk taking? Use your text and the following **InfoTrac** articles to address these questions:

DeGaston, J.F., Weed, S., & Jensen, L. (1996). Understanding gender differences in adolescent sexuality. *Adolescence, 31,* p. 217 (15).

Hubbs-Tait, L., & Garmon, L.C. (1995). The relationship of moral reasoning and AIDS knowledge to risky sexual behavior. *Adolescence, 30,* p. 549 (16).

Miller, K.S., Kotchick, B.A., Dorsey, S., Forehand, R., & Ham, A. (1998). Family communication about sex: What are parents saying and are their adolescents listening? *Family Planning Perspectives, 30,* p. 218 (5).

Werner-Wilson, R.J. (1998). Gender differences in adolescent sexual attitudes: The influence of individual and family factors. *Adolescence, 33,* p. 519 (1).

Personality *and* Social Development *in* Adolescence

Chapter Objectives

After studying Chapter Thirteen of the text, you should be able to:

* describe the function of rites of passage in non-industrial societies.

* describe how adolescent self-concept is more differentiated than that of younger children.

* discuss gender differences in how adolescents create an adult identity.

* compare Erikson's fifth psychosocial stage, identity versus role confusion, to his sixth stage, intimacy versus isolation.

* discuss why adolescents today may have particular difficulty in creating an adult identity.

* clarify the role that exploration and commitment play in adolescent identity.

* distinguish between behavioral and emotional autonomy and discuss how both are achieved during adolescence.

* chart the typical course of adolescent parent relationships through the period of adolescence.

* discuss the relationship between family conflict and adolescent autonomy.

* distinguish between mother-adolescent relationships and father-adolescent relationships.

* describe how parent-adolescent relationships vary according to culture.

* describe the adjustment challenges that usually accompany transitions to middle school and high school.

* describe typical adolescent attitudes about attending school.

* discuss reasons for the differences in achievement motivation between male and female adolescents.

* describe the special problems of minorities in high school.

* profile the typical high school dropout.

* describe why so many adolescents have difficulty making informed career decisions.

* evaluate the problems and challenges facing young men and women who choose nontraditional careers.

* discuss the special vocational problems of ethnic and racial minorities.

* discuss the issues surrounding adolescent part-time employment.

* summarize basic statistics concerning adolescent drug use and abuse.

* describe the various pressures on adolescents to experiment with illegal drugs.

* profile the "typical" delinquent and his/her per and family environment.

Study Questions

Consider these questions **before** you read the chapter:

1. What rites of passage exist in industrialized countries such as the United States and Canada?

2. Do adolescents view themselves as children or adults?

3. Why do so many adolescents feel self-conscious and insecure?

4. Why do male adolescents generally feel more self-confident than do female adolescents?

5. According to Erikson, what is the relationship between identity and intimacy?

6. Why did Erikson suggest that achieving an adult identity is the greatest challenge facing adolescents?

7. Why is exploration of alternatives so important during adolescence?

8. Why do adults insist that adolescents eventually commit to a particular life path?

9. How can an adolescent become an individual while staying emotionally connected to others?

10. How does the parent-child relationship change during adolescence?

11. Compare the relative influence on adolescents of parents and peers.

12. How do parents change their parenting style as their adolescent matures?

13. What do adolescents and their parents argue about?

14. How does middle school (junior high school) differ from elementary school?

15. How is high school different from middle school?

16. Do male and female adolescents have different achievement needs?

17. What is the profile of the typical high school dropout?

18. What misunderstandings do many adolescents have about career planning?

19. How have career opportunities changed for females over the past twenty years?

20. What are the pros and cons of part-time employment for adolescents?

21. Describe the relationship between socioeconomic status and delinquency.

Study Questions Review

After you have studied Chapter Thirteen, fill in this section.

1. What rites of passage exist in industrialized countries such as the United States and Canada?

_____
_____
_____
_____
_____
_____

2. Do adolescents view themselves as children or adults? Explain.

_____

_____

_____

_____

_____

_____

_____

_____

3. Why do so many adolescents feel self-conscious and insecure?

_____

_____

_____

_____

_____

_____

_____

_____

_____

4. Why do male adolescents generally feel more self-confident than do female adolescents?

_____

_____

_____

_____

_____

_____

5. According to Erikson, what is the relationship between identity and intimacy?

_____

_____

_____

_____

_____

6. Why did Erikson suggest that achieving an adult identity is the greatest challenge facing adolescents?

_____

_____

_____

_____

_____

_____

_____

_____

7. Why is exploration of alternatives so important during adolescence?

_____

_____

_____

_____

_____

_____

_____

_____

8. Why do adults insist that adolescents eventually commit to a particular life path?

_____

_____

_____

_____

_____

_____

9. How can an adolescent become an individual while staying emotionally connected to others?

_____

_____

_____

_____
_____
_____
_____
_____
_____

10. How does the parent-child relationship change during adolescence?

_____
_____
_____
_____
_____
_____
_____
_____
_____

11. Compare the relative influence on adolescents of parents and peers.

_____
_____
_____
_____
_____
_____
_____
_____
_____

12. How do parents adjust their parenting style as their adolescent matures?

_____
_____
_____
_____
_____
_____
_____
_____

13. What do adolescents and their parents argue about?

_____
_____
_____
_____
_____
_____
_____
_____

14. How does middle school (junior high school) differ from elementary school?

_____
_____
_____
_____
_____
_____
_____
_____
_____

15. How is high school different from middle school?

_____
_____
_____
_____
_____
_____
_____
_____

16. Do male and female adolescents have different achievement needs? Explain.

_____
_____
_____
_____
_____
_____

17. What is the profile of the typical high school dropout?

_____
_____
_____
_____
_____
_____
_____
_____

18. What misunderstandings do many adolescents have about career planning?

_____
_____
_____
_____
_____
_____
_____
_____

19. How have career opportunities changed for females over the past twenty years?

_____
_____
_____
_____
_____
_____
_____
_____

20. What are the pros and cons of part-time employment for adolescents?

_____
_____
_____
_____
_____

_____
_____
_____
_____

21. Describe the relationship between socioeconomic status and delinquency.

_____
_____
_____
_____
_____
_____

Important Terms and Concepts

Match the term to its definition below

A. Pseudomaturity __
B. Exploration (crisis) __
C. Identity versus role confusion __
D. Identity __
E. Intimacy versus isolation __
F. Identity diffusion __
G. Emotional autonomy __
H. Identity foreclosure __
I. Commitment __
J. Identity moratorium __
K. Identity achievement __
L. Behavioral autonomy __

Definitions

1. Erikson's fifth stage of psychosocial development, associated with adolescence

2. The sense of knowing who you are

3. The premature entrance into adulthood, which involves taking on adult roles before one is ready.

4. In psychosocial theory, making a decision concerning some question involved in identity formation and following a plan of action reflecting this decision

5. An identity status resulting in confusion, aimlessness, and a sense of emptiness

6. An identity status marked by a premature identity decision

7. An identity status in which a person is actively searching for an identity

8. An identity status in which a person has developed a solid, personal identity

9. Erikson's sixth psychosocial stage, occurring during young adulthood, focusing on the ability to form close relationships

10. In psychosocial theory, a time in which a person actively faces and questions aspects of his or her own identity.

11. Shifting away from the emotional dependency on parents and forming new relationships.

12. Being able to behave competently when on one's own.

Answers

A. 3	B. 10	C. 1
D. 2	E. 9	F. 5
G. 11	H. 6	I. 4
J. 7	K. 8	L. 12

Self-test: Multiple Choice

1. The stage of psychosocial development Erikson associates with adolescence emphasizes
a. conformity.
b. insecurity.
c. independence.
d. identity.

2. The stage Erikson associates with young adulthood emphasizes
a. the desire for independence.
b. the tendency to conform.
c. the need for security.
d. the ability to participate in close relationships.

3. Who described adolescence as a time of "storm and stress"
a. Erikson.
b. Piaget.
c. G. Stanley Hall.
d. Kohlberg.

4. Women are more likely than men to invest their identities in
a. relationships.
b. stocks
c. success.
d. education.

5. Along with forging an adult identity, another key challenge of adolescence is
a. finding a part time job.
b. being popular.
c. separating from one's family.
d. conforming to peer expectations.

6. Which phrase best describes the change in parent-child communication during adolescence?
a. complete break
b. total stability
c. bad faith
d. gradual renegotiation

7. Adolescents differ from their parents mainly in their views about
a. politics.
b. religion.
c. education.
d. sex and drugs.

8. Which one of the following is a nontraditional career for women?
a. librarian
b. doctor
c. schoolteacher
d. secretary

9. Susceptibility to peer pressure peaks at about what age?
a. 12
b. 14
c. 16
d. 18

10. In the last decade, high school coursework has become more
a. watered down.
b. rigorous.
c. mathematical.
d. controversial.

11. Minimum competency tests ensure that
a. each graduate has basic skills.
b. minority students are fairly treated.
c. students with special needs receive remediation.
d. critical thinking skills are taught.

12. Most part-time jobs held by teenagers
a. provide useful training and skills.
b. are related to eventual career choices.
c. are dull and boring.
d. provide excellent salaries.

13. The most frequently used drug by teenagers is
a. alcohol
b. marijuana
c. nicotine
d. cocaine

14. A major predictor of dropping out of high school is
a. having a part-time job.
b. being poor.
c. coming from a small family.
d. all of the above.

15. Delinquents generally are
a. impulsive
b. manipulative
c. resentful
d. all of the above

16. More than anything else, adolescents value
a. good grades
b. video games
c. vocational guidance
d. freedom

Self-test: True-False

__1. The search for personal identity is completed before adulthood.

__2. Most adolescents report having good relationships with, and positive feelings about, their parents.

__3. Teenage girls are more likely than boys to hide their true feelings.

198

___4. Adolescents perceive their peers as being more knowledgeable than their parents.

___5. For most teenagers, adolescence is a period of "storm and stress."

___6. Younger adolescents are more susceptible to peer influence than older adolescents.

___7. Mid-adolescence is the most trying period for parent-child relationships.

___8. Boys in mid-adolescence are more committed to intimate relationships with friends than are girls.

___9. Sometimes career choice is determined by chance.

___10. Today, women are well-represented in business as chief executives.

___11. Poorer teenagers are more likely to be employed than those from more affluent families.

___12. Girls generally do better in elementary school than boys.

___13. The common thread linking most minority youth is poverty.

___14. Most delinquents continue to pursue a life of crime as adults.

Answers

Multiple Choice

1. D	9. B
2. D	10. B
3. C	11. A
4. A	12. C
5. C	13. A
6. D	14. B
7. D	15. D
8. B	16. D

True-False

1. F	8. F
2. T	9. T
3. T	10. F
4. F	11. F
5. F	12. T
6. T	13. T
7. T	14. F

Challenge Questions

1. Evaluate your own personal identity! How would you describe yourself? How do others see you? What life goals are you pursuing? What do you believe in?

_____
_____
_____
_____
_____
_____
_____
_____
_____
_____
_____
_____

2. How can we understand the apparent hypocrisy of parents who forbid their children to do the very things they did when they were younger? Should parents let their children learn from their own mistakes or try to protect them from their occasional poor judgment?

_____
_____
_____
_____
_____
_____
_____
_____

3. Are most secondary schools getting the job done? Given the amount of time children spend in school, what do they have to show for it? How could schools be improved, if you were in charge?

_____
_____
_____
_____
_____
_____
_____
_____
_____
_____

_____
_____
_____
_____
_____

4. Some maintain that there is no such thing as a bad child. How do delinquents become delinquents? Are they born or made that way?

_____
_____
_____
_____
_____
_____
_____
_____
_____
_____
_____
_____
_____

Chapter Activities

1. Interview two working adults, one male and one female, about how they chose their career or profession. Inquire about the role played by their education, part-time jobs, parents, their knowledge about their eventual job, and the role of chance. Compare their experiences, and report your findings.

2. Find newspaper articles about teenage violence, including recent episodes of violence in high schools. What do the teenagers described in the articles have in common? What seem to be the key risk factors that lead youth to behave antisocially?

3. Why did Erik Erikson consider identity formation to be the key developmental challenge of adolescence? Why did Erikson emphasize the importance of exploration of alternatives during adolescence? Does the course of identity formation differ for males and females? Use your text (chapter 13) and the following **InfoTrac** articles to address these questions:
Kidwell, J.S., Dunham, R.M., Bacho, R.A., Pastorino, E., & Portes, P.R. (1995). Adolescent identity exploration: A test of Erikson's theory of transitional crisis. *Adolescence, 30*, p. 785 (9).
Lytle, L.J., Bakken, L., & Romig, C. (1997). Adolescent female identity development. *Sex Roles: A Journal of Research, 37*, p. 175 (11).